The World of TomorroW

GALLEY PRESS

Contents

Author
Robin Kerrod

Designer
John Strange

First published in USA 1980
by Mayflower Books, Inc,
575 Lexington Avenue, New York, New York

Designed and produced by
Grisewood & Dempsey Limited
141-143 Drury Lane, London WC2
© Grisewood and Dempsey Limited 1980

Color separations by Newsele Litho Ltd, Milan, Italy
Printed and bound by Vallardi Industrie Grafiche
S.p.A., Milan, Italy

LOC No. 80-82296

ISBN 0-8317-9493-3

Introduction

Not so very long ago the way people lived changed very little from year to year – even from century to century. They were primarily farmers, whose lives were geared to the rhythm of nature. Then, in the 18th century, the development of the steam engine launched an Industrial Revolution. Machines were built to take over the work which had been done by hand. People flocked from the countryside into the towns to work in factories. Machines invaded business, transport, the home and farming. By the end of the 19th century mechanization had laid the foundations of our present age.

The March of Progress

The first half of the present century was a time of unprecedented expansion in every area of human achievement. The cities grew outwards and upwards as architects exploited skyscraper technology. The home itself became equipped with numerous labour-saving gadgets to reduce the household chores. Health and life expectancy improved thanks to the discovery of new medicines such as antibiotics and sulpha drugs. People became increasingly mobile as mass production brought the car within their reach. Fuel for cars was abundant, for new oil fields were being found faster than they could be developed. From oil the chemical industry manufactured all manner of new products like dyes, explosives, synthetic drugs, insecticides and plastics. No-one worried that one day oil might run out for there would be inexhaustible supplies of the newly discovered nuclear power to take its place.

Problems of Expansion

However, by the 1960s it was becoming apparent that the unchecked expansion of the preceding years had brought with it a host of problems. The world population was soaring, and food production was lagging behind. The skies, the rivers, the seas and the landscape were becoming increasingly polluted. Demand for oil was becoming so great that it appeared that supplies might be exhausted by the end of the century. Many other raw materials were also being consumed at an alarming rate. The prospects of unlimited nuclear power dimmed as the problems of radioactive wastes and the shortage of uranium began to be realized.

But then the tide began to turn. Governments began to do something about the environment. They began to finance projects to develop alternative forms of energy and to back conservation on a larger scale. Views of the Earth taken from outer space somehow emphasized that we must take greater care of our beautiful planet. Space technology was beginning to bring us benefits, improving the reliability of weather forecasting and intercontinental communications, aiding mineral prospecting and vastly increasing our knowledge, not only of our own planet, but also of the universe as a whole.

The Technological Revolution

The need to miniaturize components for space satellites led to what is perhaps one of the most remarkable achievements yet – the development of the silicon chip, or microprocessor. If forecasts are to be believed, the chip will bring about, within a decade, a revolution in our way of life such as the world has never known.

Space technology and the microprocessor are just two of the things that will increasingly affect and improve our lives in the years to come. We know the problems facing us and we already have the knowledge and technology to overcome them. This is what the book is all about – the problems we face and the means of overcoming them. In almost every aspect of human life there are convincing signs that the future will be rewarding.

A New World

Undoubtedly the face of the Earth will change as the increasing population demands more living space, and interconnected super-cities may one day span the globe. People may also be housed in sea cities on the continental shelves of the oceans. Inland areas are likely to be given over mainly to intensive agriculture and water catchment. Intercity transport will increasingly be by flying trains, suspended and propelled by magnetic waves. Electricity will probably become virtually the only form of power, since the internal combustion engine, wasteful of energy and creator of pollution, will almost certainly be banned.

The fossil fuels of today will be used for their true worth, as organic raw materials. These and other raw materials, may be recycled on a large scale. Electricity will come from renewable sources such as sunshine, wind and tides. The greatest breakthrough in energy production will come when we tap, in nuclear fusion reactors, the fundamental energy that runs the universe. Controlled nuclear fusion should provide us with abundant energy for centuries upon centuries. By then we may well have forsaken our earthbound existence and founded new civilizations in space.

Population

Before the Industrial Revolution got under way in the 1700s, most people in the world were farmers and lived in small communities. They were, to a large extent, self-supporting. But the Industrial Revolution changed all this and started a drift from the country to the city, a trend which has continued ever since. In the United States, for example, only 6 out of every 100 people lived in towns in 1800. Today 75 out of every 100 people do so.

Unless scattered communities are self-sufficient, they pose problems in transport and communications. As energy becomes scarcer, only centralized transport systems will make economic sense. The village and small country town may well vanish because they are no longer economic units. They occupy a large area for the number of people they support, and land is becoming increasingly scarce.

The People Boom

The rapidly expanding world population is causing many problems. In 1750 the world population stood at about 800 million. It took 150 years (to 1900) for the population to double. But it then took only 70 years (to 1970) for the population to double yet again. Already the world population is nearing 4500 million. If present trends continue, the world population will double again in less than 40 years. By AD 2020 it could be approaching 10 000 million.

The phenomenal increase in population results from the difference between birth and death rates. About 250 births occur in the world every minute, but only about 100 people die. Improvements in medicine, health care and education mean that fewer babies die at birth, fewer people die from disease, and old people live longer.

Given that the world's food resources are limited, will we be able to feed the population in the year 2020? Using modern farming methods it takes about 0.4 hectares (1 acre) of land to produce enough food for one person. The area of the world's land surface for farming is about 46 million square kilometres (18 million square miles), which could support a population of 10 000 million people. So even with existing farming practice the 2020 population could be fed.

Assuming modest advances in agricultural methods, it is likely that the world could support a population as high as 15 000 million. Such a population might be achieved by the middle of the next century. What happens then? Fortunately, the signs are that the present population explosion may soon slow down and that the population will steady between 10 000 and 15 000 million.

A steadying of the population will come about as a result of increased world wealth; as people become more affluent and better educated, they tend to limit the size of their families. This is much easier to do today than in the past for many methods of birth control, or contraception, are now available. The birth rate in the advanced industrial societies of the West, already low, is still declining. In the United States and in most European countries, the birth rate has now dropped to such a low level that it will soon result in zero population growth, with as many people being born as dying.

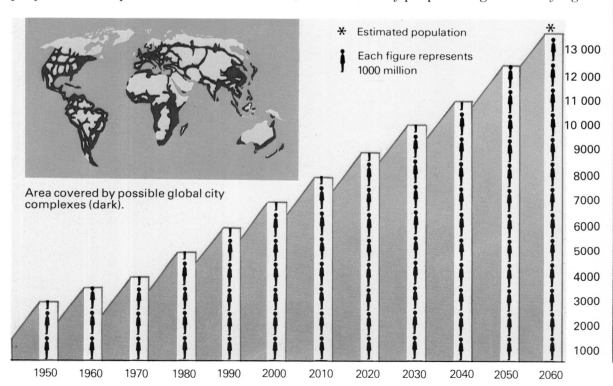

Area covered by possible global city complexes (dark).

* Estimated population

Each figure represents 1000 million

13 000
12 000
11 000
10 000
9000
8000
7000
6000
5000
4000
3000
2000
1000

1950 1960 1970 1980 1990 2000 2010 2020 2030 2040 2050 2060

High Living

Whatever happens to the population, in the years ahead cities will almost certainly grow bigger, while the countryside grows emptier. As the small town, village and hamlet disappear, so will the sprawling network of lanes and roads between them. All this land may well be returned to agriculture, for every piece of suitable land will have to be intensively cultivated. Eventually even main intercity highways will be replaced by high-speed monorail links.

The cities of the future will not be very different from many of today's advanced cities, dominated by high-rise apartment buildings and skyscraper office blocks. They will be built of similar materials – mainly reinforced concrete and glass. But the greatest difference is likely to be in scale, for tomorrow's cities will probably boast tower structures several kilometres high. By contrast, in 1980 the world's tallest building, the Sears Tower in Chicago, stood at only 443 metres (1453 ft).

Design studies have indicated that such vast towers are technically feasible. One design has a tower 3 kilometres (2 miles) high and 200 metres (650 ft) square. It

Above: New York at night. Skyscrapers are likely to be built higher and higher as building space becomes scarcer.

Right: Interconnected tower cities like this could span the continents next century. They will be able to house enormous populations yet take up minimal surface area. The technical knowledge for building such structures already exists, and existing materials such as reinforced concrete and glass could be used. Inter-city communication would be by means of advanced passenger conveyor systems through interconnecting tubes. The ground areas around the towers could be used for recreation.

10

Left: The vast glass roof of this school building forms part of the solar heating and cooling system which warms the school in winter and air-conditions it in summer. The heat of the Sun is extracted by the panels through which water is circulated. The circulating water transfers its heat to a heat exchanger which provides heat for space heating or air-conditioning.

Below left: A solar-powered heat pump gathers the Sun's energy in a solar collector and converts it to heat energy. The heat is used to heat or cool a house. The system contains a phase-change material (PCM) which is capable of storing surplus heat energy for use during the night or on cloudy days. Surplus heat can be used for hothouses or swimming pools as well.

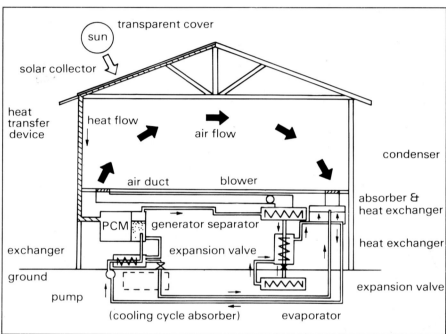

Below: In the future you may be able to take an ultrasonic bath in this curious 'washer egg'. The machine is designed to wash, massage and dry the body so that it is ultraclean and relaxed.

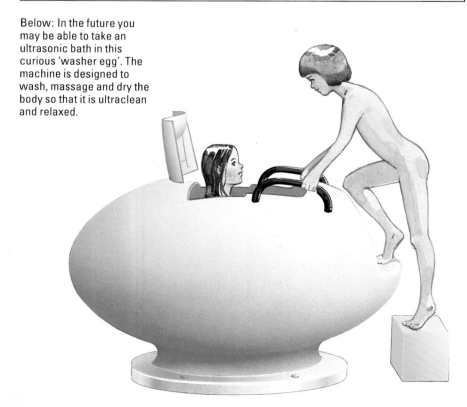

could house some 250 000 people and include not only family apartments, but also shops, restaurants, offices, factories and so on. However, many people think such tower cities are socially and psychologically undesirable.

While some tower cities might be built in isolation, others could be incorporated into supercities. Moving pedestrian walkways and high-speed mass-transit links at different levels could provide fast, efficient transport between cities. The land areas between the towers would be given over to parks and lakes. The city would also extend underground, where there would be shops, restaurants, theatres and leisure centres. Many cities are already building underground to gain much needed space, away from the traffic congestion, pollution and bad weather on the surface.

Eventually, tower cities could grow along the high-speed monorail networks that link them, in a ribbon development that could span the continents.

Home Comforts

Cloud-high tower cities are still a long way off and for some time to come most people will continue to live in houses not much different from those of today. But these homes will be built to more exacting standards and will be more efficiently insulated so that they waste less energy.

The family house of the future will almost certainly be designed with energy conservation as a major feature. This will affect the siting of the house, its layout and overall structural design. Insulating materials such as compressed volcanic ash, rigid plastic foams and even paper honeycombs are likely to be used for the inner walls instead of concrete blocks. Solar collector panels can be installed on the roof. Even in relatively cool climates these can reduce water heating bills by up to 50 per cent. The collector is essentially a blackened plate containing channels through which

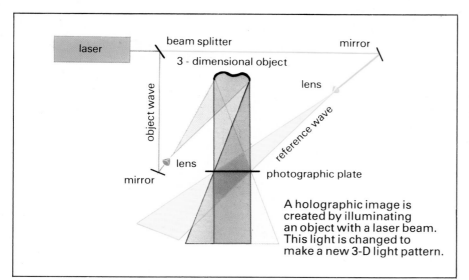

A holographic image is created by illuminating an object with a laser beam. This light is changed to make a new 3-D light pattern.

Above: Among the many entertainment devices that will be available in the future will be the true three-dimensional moving picture. Early experiments with 3D films required the audience to wear special glasses with different coloured lenses. But true 3D viewing is promised by recent advances in holography. Holography uses a laser beam to create an image. The photographic plate carries 3D information in peculiar wave patterns, not as a recognizable picture.

Below: Only when a laser beam is shone through the pattern on the photographic plate does a 3D image appear. By modifying the holographic system, 3D 'movies' have already been shown to be feasible.

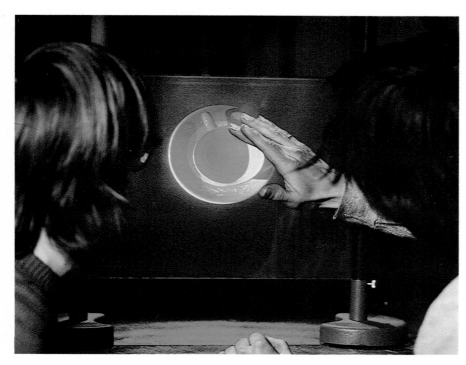

Left: Viewphones are likely to be commonplace before the end of the century, though they may well look different from this one. They would almost certainly be linked with a master audiovisual communications centre which modern homes could then have.

water is circulated. It absorbs heat from the Sun, which is removed by water. The water circulates through a heat-exchange unit in a storage tank which feeds water to the domestic hot-water cistern. A glass plate fits over the collector and acts like a miniature greenhouse to keep in the heat.

Heat-exchange units will also be incorporated in the waste-water disposal system. These will use any heat in the waste-water to preheat water going into the domestic hot-water supply, or warm a reservoir of earth, wet sand or concrete set in the ground beneath the house. Efficient heat pumps could then extract the heat later as required.

Isolated buildings far away from mains power sources will also be equipped with a methane digester to supply gas for heating and cooking. This will ferment any unwanted organic matter (human, animal and vegetable wastes) into methane, the main gas in the natural gas now used for heating and cooking. The sludge remaining after fermentation will make an excellent fertilizer. A house in a breezy location might also use a windmill to provide energy.

This kind of house, using the renewable energy resources of the Sun and the wind and recycling its waste products, represents what is known as alternative technology. It is a low-technology answer to many future living problems, and contrasts starkly with the high technology of tower cities, power satellites and atomic fusion reactors. However, there seems every reason to suppose that both low and high technologies will have as large a part to play in tomorrow's world as they do in today's. The high could have its place in the great global city complexes and the low in the isolated agricultural, water-pumping and communications-relay stations that will be scattered in the otherwise uninhabited country areas.

The Electronic Home

The ingenious device known as the microprocessor (page 59) will probably bring about as big a revolution in the home as it will in industry. Every household could eventually possess its own computer to cope with the day-to-day running of the home, which could link up with more powerful external computers when necessary. The chances are that it would be voice-activated, but respond only to the voices of people in the household.

When correctly programmed, the home computer could take over routine tasks like ordering new supplies of food as they run out, paying bills, storing all kinds of personal information like favourite recipes, names and addresses, and details of the bank balance and insurance policies.

The computer would be incorporated into a master electronic control console linked to audiovisual outlets in various rooms. These would compromise a keyboard and TV screen on which would be displayed TV programmes, electronic newspapers (like the teletext of today), educational courses, restaurant menus, train times, books available in the local library, and so on. Mail would also be electronic. People would type out a letter on the video screen and despatch it to an address. There it would go into a memory store for recall later, or be simultaneously copied by a high-speed print-out unit.

The TV screen for the family could be wall size, made possible by the development of a flat screen. Later would come the 3D viewer, based on the principles of laser holography, which would conjure up a true three-dimensional image in the air.

A New Atlantis

The oceans cover more than twice as much of the Earth's surface as the continents. The drawback is that the average depth of the oceans is about 4000 metres (1300 feet).

1 Flats

2 Ventilation ducts

3 Public buildings

4 Industrial complexes

5 Generating machinery and servicing areas

6 City wall

7 Reinforced concrete pile foundations

Above: Self-contained 'Sea Cities' could provide an offshore home for many people in the future. The main activities of the city would take place inside the encircling wall.

The sheltered internal lagoon would provide a perfect setting for restaurants, theatres and individual housing.

The design shows a city some 500 metres (1600 ft) across, with an encircling wall some 55 metres (180 ft) high.

Around each continent there is only a narrow, relatively shallow region that gently slopes downwards away from the shoreline. This is known as the continental shelf which on average is about 80 kilometres (50 miles) wide. Together these shelves add up to the equivalent of about 15 per cent of the existing land area.

The depth of the continental shelf varies from place to place, but averages no more than about 130 metres (450 ft). It is often considerably shallower. We already have the technology to cope with such depths, as for example in offshore oil exploration and production (page 49). Some habitats could be built underwater in regions where the seabed is being farmed (page 22). Most activities however would probably take place above the surface. There are plans to build artificial islands from material dredged from the surrounding seabed.

These artificial islands would be ideal sites for industrial activities and power plants, being away from centres of population. In shallower regions closer to the shore new cities could be built to house tens of thousands of people.

Designs for such a 'Sea City' have been made by a group of architects sponsored by Pilkington Brothers, the glass manufacturers. Their Sea City is like a floating amphitheatre built around a central lagoon. The main construction material for the basic structure is reinforced concrete, and glass and GRP (glass-fibre reinforced plastic) are extensively used for the super-structure. All these materials are immune to erosion or other damage by the sea. A high encircling wall, built on piles driven into the sea-bed, would deflect prevailing winds up and over the city, providing shelter for the people inside.

Future Food

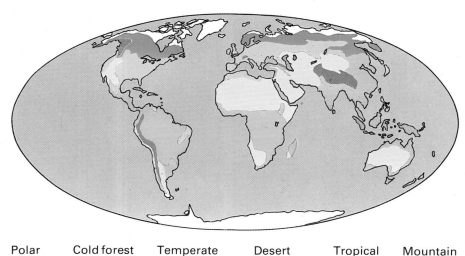

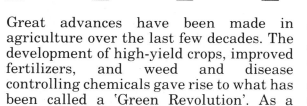

Polar	Cold forest	Temperate	Desert	Tropical	Mountain
☐	◼	◻	◻	◻	◼

Great advances have been made in agriculture over the last few decades. The development of high-yield crops, improved fertilizers, and weed and disease controlling chemicals gave rise to what has been called a 'Green Revolution'. As a result, wheat yields doubled in the 1950s and doubled again in the 1960s.

New strains of plants have been produced by selective cross-breeding of different strains and by artificial mutations. Mutations are brought about by irradiating the plants with gamma rays. This alters their genetic make-up and produces different varieties of plants in subsequent generations. Some of these mutations eventually lead to better crops. Selective breeding has improved the quality of livestock in an equally spectacular manner. Cows give more milk, pigs fatten more quickly, and beef cattle produce better quality meat faster than ever before.

In the future the intensive or factory-farming methods of today will be practised on a much larger scale. Animals which are kept in a carefully controlled environment will be automatically fed precise amounts of the right food producing larger quantities of cheap meat, though many people consider the method inhumane.

Helping Nature

Improved cattle can be produced by means of artificial insemination. The deep-frozen sperm from one prize bull can now be used to fertilize thousands of cows.

A novel technique to improve animal breeding is now in the experimental stage. This is embryo-transplanting. A particularly fine cow is given hormone treatment to make it produce several eggs instead of one. These are then fertilized, and when

Above: The climate of a region largely determines the kind of crops and livestock, if any, that can be raised. Vast areas of the world are hot or cold wastelands where virtually nothing can grow.

Above: Meaty-looking chunks of soya protein are now widely used as an alternative or supplement to real meat. Soya beans are treated with a solvent to extract the protein-rich oil from which the protein is then isolated. The protein concentrate is then dissolved and 'spun' into fibres which are blended and flavoured and bulked into chunks. Soyafood could provide a plentiful source of protein to enrich diets in poorer countries.

16

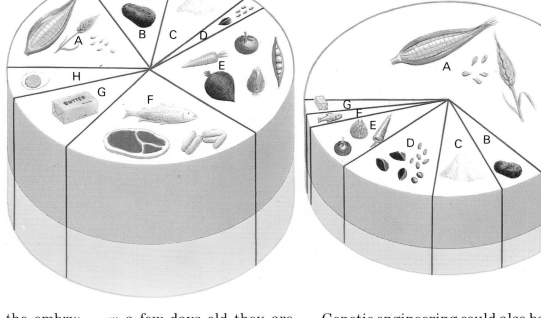

the embryos are a few days old they are removed from the 'donor' cow and stored in a suitable medium. They can then be implanted in other healthy but less fine cows. The 'foster' cows from then on undergo a normal pregnancy.

In time, it is thought that prize animals may be cloned. Cloning is a method of asexual reproduction from a single parent. It is at present in its infancy and by 1980 had been successfully carried out only in frogs and partly in mice. Normally an egg cell starts dividing to produce a new organism only when it has been fertilized and contains a mixture of the genes of both parents. In cloning, a cell is made to divide without fertilization and so the new organism has exactly the same genes as its single parent. It is an exact replica of that parent. Selected cattle may one day be cloned by replacing the nucleus in the egg cell of a foster cow with the nucleus of a cell from a suitable donor.

Genetic Engineering

Improvements in the breeding of livestock and plants may eventually be brought about by genetic engineering (see page 27). By altering the genes themselves, favourable characteristics could be introduced and unfavourable ones removed. Experiments are already proceeding that could bring about a fundamental breakthrough in crop production. The aim is to induce major cereal crops such as wheat to fix nitrogen from the atmosphere and convert it to a form that the plants can use to make proteins. Plants such as peas and beans do this and, as a result, they replenish the soil as they grow. Success with other crops would eliminate the need for the vast amounts of nitrogen fertilizers now used to nourish most major crops.

Genetic engineering could also be used to give crops other desirable characteristics. They may be 'tailored' to fit a particular environment. A heavy-cropping variety of wheat, for example, might be genetically altered into a strain that thrives in hot countries and resists drought. While new strains of plants have already been produced using genes altered by radiation, it is still very much a hit-and-miss process. Genetic engineering is much more precise.

Controlling Pests and Diseases

Genetic engineering could be used to curb plant disease. The plants themselves could be genetically altered to make them more resistant, and the disease germs – bacteria, fungi and viruses – could be modified to make them less harmful or even harmless.

At the moment control over diseases, insects and other pests is achieved mainly by chemicals. This has some serious drawbacks. For one thing, some chemicals are poisonous to living things other than the pest or disease they are intended to control. Another drawback is that pests and diseases often become resistant to a chemical by developing new strains that are immune to it. For example, in the 1940s DDT almost wiped out the mosquitoes that cause malaria in topical regions. But these insects are now as active as ever and are resistant to DDT.

To prevent these kinds of problems, researchers are aiming at a less hazardous and more lasting method of control – biological control. This has already been done successfully using two methods which may eventually be effective against most insect pests.

One method involves sterilizing millions of male mosquitoes by chemical treatment. They are then released into infested regions where they mate with female mosquitoes, but because they are sterilized no young are produced. If sterilized males are released over a period of a few months the mosquito population can be entirely eliminated. This technique has already been used with great success in both North and South America. The same method has also prevented screw-worm and fruit fly epidemics in the United States; in these cases, radiation was used to sterilize the males.

A second method requires the use of a synthetic hormone to achieve insect control. Called a juvenile hormone (JH), it is applied to an insect larva and prevents it from becoming an adult. Tests in more than thirty countries have shown that spraying synthetic JH on mosquito breeding grounds can eliminate the pests by preventing them from growing and reproducing. It seems unlikely that mosquitoes and other pests will develop resistance to synthetic JH because it mimics their natural JH. Unlike other pesticides, JH only attacks the insect it is meant to, so harmless or beneficial insects are safe.

Making the Deserts Bloom
Another way of increasing food production is to put more land under cultivation. Most suitable land is already being used for farming, but there are vast areas of land available that lack but one thing – rainfall.

Arid and semi-arid deserts cover over 40 per cent of the Earth's land surface. Since civilization began about 10 000 years ago, some 9 million square kilometres (3½ million square miles) of land have become desert. Desert areas are still increasing year by year, partly because the climate is changing but also because of a short-sighted approach to agriculture.

In primitive nomadic agriculture, farmers clear the land of trees and other vegetation. They grow crops until the soil is exhausted and then move on. The land is then overgrazed by livestock until only unpalatable thornbush, cactus and mesquite remain; goats may take over and completely clear the land of plant life. When drought occurs, the topsoil dries out and, with nothing to anchor it, is blown away by the wind. Careless agriculture created desert in the former Fertile Crescent in the Middle East. It caused the vast dust bowls of the Great Plains of the United States and the present advance of the Sahara Desert. Careless irrigation of land can also render land unsuitable for agriculture. Unless there is proper drainage, the salts in irrigated water can build up in the soil as the water evaporates, until the soil becomes too salty for any plants to grow and the land becomes barren.

Ecologists are confident they can eventually win back some of the desert for agriculture. Where there is still soil to take roots, desert can be reclaimed. A concerted world-wide effort to do this is already under way as a result of the first United Nations Conference on Desertification held in 1977, in which 95 nations took part.

Schemes for growing crops in the deserts are also under way. Many are developments of what is called soil-less culture. Plants are raised in huge enclosures made of plastic sheet. The plants are supplied with a solution containing the nutrients absent from the desert soil. This kind of hydroponic agriculture will be increasingly used in the years ahead.

Perhaps the most ambitious scheme that has been proposed for desert agriculture is one using a self-inflating flying air-craft. It is designed to hover in the air over the desert and create a mini-climate by controlling the air temperature and pressure. Clouds are formed and water vapour condenses so that it falls as rain.

Controlling the Weather
Meteorologists still know too little about the complex nature of weather to be able to predict that some day weather will be brought under control. But they can now forecast the weather more accurately, especially in the short term. Information satellites and remote weather-monitoring stations allow them to warn people when storms, hail, hurricanes and frost are due so that suitable precautions can be taken.

The vast tracts of hot desert that cover much of the Earth's surface are barren wildernesses at present (below). But it may be possible to change them into productive regions for growing crops and raising livestock. The idea is to float above the huge inflated structures (right). These can create a microclimate in which temperature and humidity can be controlled and suited to the growth of vegetation.

There has been some success in controlling weather locally by cloud-seeding. This is usually done by aircraft which drop silver iodine flares into the clouds. The tiny particles of silver iodine act as nucleii around which the water vapour in the cloud condenses into droplets. The droplets grow until they are large enough to fall as rain. Dry ice, or solid carbon dioxide, is also sometimes used in cloud-seeding experiments.

This technique can, in some instances, induce rain to fall in regions stricken by drought. It can also prevent the formation of hailstones in thunderstorms and so prevent serious crop damage. Cloud-seeding is also practised at airports to disperse fog and it has achieved limited success in reducing the force of hurricanes.

Preventing Lightning

A similar technique has been used to prevent lightning. The thunderclouds are seeded with aluminium-coated nylon fibres. The fibres neutralize electric charges within the cloud and prevent them building up to cause a lightning bolt. The Russians are reported to have had some

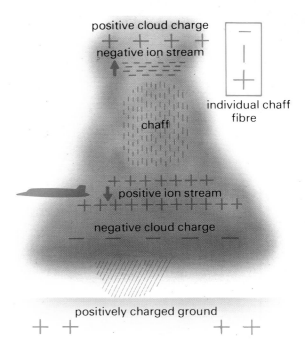

positive cloud charge

negative ion stream

individual chaff fibre

chaff

positive ion stream

negative cloud charge

positively charged ground

Above: With improved long-range forecasting, it may be possible to control freak weather in the future. Merciless drought (top) and catastrophic tornadoes are as yet beyond human control.

Thunderstorms and lightning can cause enormous harm but some success has already been achieved in controlling them. 'Bombing' thunderclouds with metallized fibre 'chaff' has proved an excellent way of switching off lighting (above). The fibres form an electrically conducting path which prevents the build-up of the very high voltages needed to cause lightning.

success in preventing thunderstorm damage by firing shells into the clouds.

Farming the Seas

Fish is an excellent all-around food both for humans and, in the form of fish meal, for animals. Since 1950 the annual catch of fish in the world has doubled to about 70 million tonnes and there is evidence that the seas are becoming overfished. Some experts believe that if present trends continue the seas could, by the 21st century, be fished out of at least the fifty or so species that are the most popular foods.

More optimistically, it has been estimated that the present catch of the popular species represents only about one thousandth of the overall fish population of the oceans. So it seems sensible to begin to catch some of the tens of thousands of other species for food. Even if some fish are unappetizing for humans, they can be made into fish meal or supply oil and vitamins for livestock feed.

Fish production can be increased by 'farming' the seas. Fish-farming, or aqua-culture, is already being practised on a small scale in many parts of the world both in inland waters and offshore. The Chinese have been expert fish farmers for some time, raising such species as quick-growing carp, while in Thailand the tropical fish *Tilapia* is farmed to yield over 40 tonnes per acre each year. Offshore farming of oysters and lobsters is also widely practised.

Fish farming in the future will almost certainly be done on a much larger scale. Vast areas of coastal waters could be penned off and used to rear numerous species of fish. The continental shelves may also be intensively farmed. There, fish may be kept in pens formed by barriers of bubbles which fish will not pass through. The sea cities and island industrial complexes of the future could also provide good locations for fish farming. They would warm up the surrounding waters enough to increase the rate of growth of the fish.

Normally, the spawning and fertilization of fish eggs are very haphazard, and during hatching and early growth the fish are very vulnerable to attack from predators. In fish farming, these vital stages take place in controlled conditions in fish nurseries and the fish are not released into the sea pens until they are large enough to thrive until they are harvested.

Below: Though we are still a long way from controlling the weather, we now know much more about global weather patterns, thanks to weather satellites.

Weather satellites take photographs of the cloud formations that accompany shifting air masses, and also relay other meteorological data.

Satellite observation will continue to provide meteorologists with a world-wide view of the weather situation, from which they can more accurately forecast how the weather will change. By issuing warnings of frost, floods, hurricanes and cyclones well in advance, they can help to save crops, livestock, homes and human lives.

Simple Sources

All life in the seas depends ultimately on countless minute life forms called plankton. They include plants such as algae as well as tiny animals such as protozoans, sea worms and the larvae and young of jellyfish, crabs and other crustaceans and fishes. Plankton forms the beginning of the food chain for virtually all marine life, and represents an abundant source of protein. In the future, it might be farmed directly to provide food but enormous processing plants would be required to remove it from the sea. To produce one tonne of plankton, over 1000 million litres (250 million imperial gallons) of ocean would have to be processed.

Simple organisms such as algae also feature in other schemes to produce protein foodstuffs. The simplest algae are primitive single-celled slimes and weeds. These can be processed to yield a protein-rich product termed SCP (single-celled protein). SCP can also be obtained from other simple organisms such as bacteria, yeasts and moulds. Processing of this kind is already being carried out experimentally and may be practised on a large scale by the 21st century.

Unlikely Sources

In SCP plants the live protein source is allowed to multiply or ferment in a suitable medium. After fermentation, the SCP is separated, washed and dried. It is then flavoured and textured to imitate, for example, beef steak or chicken. The most unlikely sources are used for fermentation – whey, molasses, starch, the waste liquid from paper-making and even petroleum oils. Suitable bacteria have also been found that feed on cellulose, the main substance in woody tissue. Cellulose is discarded in vast quantities at present in waste paper, straw and other agricultural waste. If large-scale cellulose processing plants come into operation, there could be a vital and renewable food store that could help solve the problem of starvation.

Right: Fish farming is practised at present only on a relatively small scale, in coastal units serviced from the surface. Future fish farms could look more like this.

They would be located not only near the coasts, but also in other shallow waters anywhere on the continental shelf. Fish of different species would be raised in separate cages on the seabed, or in the waters above them. Fish in the open water would be kept penned in by barriers of air bubbles, which would also serve to keep predators out.

The fish-farm complex could also include underwater habitats, laboratories and nurseries, where fish eggs could be fertilized and hatched under controlled conditions. It might also include machinery to process the fish when they have been harvested.

Left: Plankton is made up of tiny drifting plants and animals that form a nutritious broth in the upper layer of the sea. Directly or indirectly, plankton nourishes all the larger creatures living in the sea. Here we see a small crustacean larva and tiny floating algae.

22

Health and Medicine

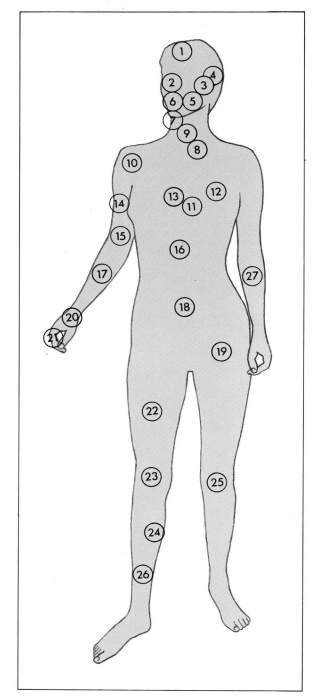

Spare-part surgery has come a long way since the early days of the wooden leg and glass eye. This has been brought about mainly by the availability of materials like titanium and plastics which the body does not reject.

Some of the parts which can already be substituted are shown in this diagram.

1 'Vitallium' skull plate
2 Plastic nose implant
3 In-the-ear hearing aid
4 Silicone plastic ear
5 Metal jaw bone
6 Dentures
7 Chin implant
8 Spitz-Holter valve to control fluid on the brain
9 Electronic larynx
10 Shoulder joint replacement
11 Heart valve replacement
12 Heart pacemaker
13 Filter preventing blood clotting in circulation to lungs
14 Dacron artery replacement
15 Elbow replacement
16 Dacron vein + artery graft
17 Metal bone plate
18 Plastic intestinal replacement
19 Hip joint replacement
20 Wrist-bone replacement
21 Finger-joint replacement
22 Thigh-bone replacement
23 Knee-joint replacement
24 Plastic artery graft
25 Artificial leg with knee and ankle movement
26 Shin
27 Artificial arm

Heart transplants, test-tube babies and laser surgery make newspaper headlines. But bionic human beings are unlikely to be with us in the near future; they still belong to the world of science fiction.

Health problems of the future will be broadly similar to those of today. For most of the world, miracle medicines and surgery will remain a dream, and for the poor, so will even the most basic medical care.

In the Third World, there is still a grim link between poverty and ill health. A poor diet, polluted water and crowded slums mean that millions do not enjoy the benefits of medical science. People suffering from malnutrition have little resistance to disease. They succumb quickly, as they always have, to epidemics of dysentry, cholera, typhoid and bilharzia. The six most common diseases in the world affect a quarter of all people in the world. For these people, the biggest advance will be in improving public health and obtaining vaccines and antibiotics.

By contrast, the health problems of the developed nations are very different, for it is not malnutrition that takes the biggest toll, but the diseases of affluence.

Overweight and under-exercised bodies place great strain on the heart and blood vessels. More than half the deaths among men in the West aged 45 to 54 result from heart and circulatory diseases caused by degenerating artery walls becoming blocked. For many, the 'cure' could result from a more relaxed life style and a better diet rather than from a miracle drug.

Spare-part surgery

Sometimes the body organs are so damaged or malformed by disease that no drugs can correct the problem. More drastic action is needed. In some cases, sophisticated surgery can help, as in 'hole-in-the-heart' operations. In others, a whole organ may have to be removed and replaced.

Organ transplants, once rare, are now performed more often and with increasing success. Hundreds of people have already been given a new lease of life in this way.

An alternative to transplanting organs from human donors lies in making them synthetically. Partly artificial hearts have been used since the 1960s, and pacemakers that stimulate the heart by giving it minute electric shocks are commonly worn inside the body by people with certain heart conditions. Damaged heart valves can be replaced with ones made of specially treated carbon or plastics such as polyurethane. Diseased blood vessels can also be repaired using materials like

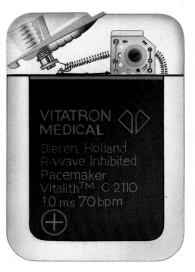

VITATRON MEDICAL
Dieren, Holland
R-wave Inhibited
Pacemaker
Vitalith™ C 2110
1.0 ms 70 bpm

Heart disease is one of the biggest killers in advanced societies. A common complaint is the weakness of the electric pulses that cause the heart to beat. This can be treated by implanting a heart pacemaker (shown actual size) in the chest cavity to stimulate the heart artificially. It comprises a battery-powered pulse generator sealed inside a titanium capsule.

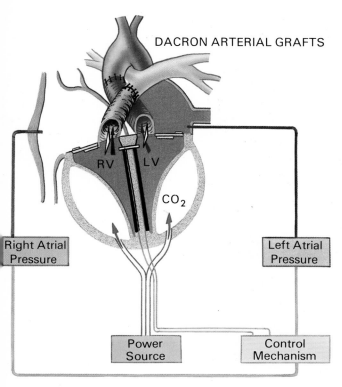

DACRON ARTERIAL GRAFTS

RV LV

CO$_2$

Right Atrial Pressure

Left Atrial Pressure

Power Source

Control Mechanism

Dacron, Teflon and silicone rubber. These are inert substances that do not generally react with the body's fluids and are not usually rejected by its defences.

Artificial Hearts

The ultimate solution to many heart troubles lies in the fully artificial heart. Some prototypes have already kept research animals alive for months. The normal pumping action of the heart muscles is done by a compressed-air pump. However, this sort of device is still too crude for human use. Tests are being carried out with electric-powered models that may be more suitable. Indications are that reliable units will be available by 1990 and that thousands of people will be using artificial hearts by the turn of the century.

Research is also proceeding with the building of artificial heart-lung machines and the making of synthetic skin and blood. An artificial blood with a substance called fluosol in it has already been tested in human beings. It can hold vast quantities of oxygen and is ideal for use during surgery when massive transfusions are needed.

Although the complete bionic person is not yet with us, it has been estimated that hardly a single organ in the body will be irreplaceable by the 21st century.

Curing Cancer

Cancer is the term for a host of diseases in which 'rogue' cells in the body invade and destroy healthy tissue. Cancer is the great 'mystery killer' of the 20th century. Smoking, radiation and certain irritant chemicals are known to be linked with it. But as often as not it seems to arise spontaneously.

There are signs, however, that a cure for cancer, or at least some cancers, is possible. Biologists have isolated enzymes that cause cancer cells to form; they have also found compounds that block the action of these enzymes.

Though this method shows promise, the cure for cancer still represents the greatest hurdle of modern medicine. One line of experimentation is to make cancer cells convert back into healthy tissue. If a drug can be produced that 'trains' cells how to behave normally again, rather than kills them, the body's natural controls could cure cancer cells.

The Wonder Drugs

One of the most crucial medical problems is the need to eradicate, or at least contain, infectious diseases. This is especially true in the Third World where epidemics sweep rapidly through entire populations.

Antibiotics – the most famous of which is penicillin – destroy bacteria that invade the body. Killers such as pneumonia and meningitis can be beaten today, provided they are treated in time. In the future, the big breakthrough in antibiotics will not lie in developing new ones but in making the ones that already exist available to as many people in the world as possible.

Far left: Diagram of the first artificial heart used in a human being in 1969. It is primitive in comparison with the ones projected for the future but it showed the way ahead.

The pumping action was achieved by the flexing of a diaphragm by means of compressed carbon dioxide (CO$_2$). Left and right atrial pressure is pressure necessary to the two upper cavities of the heart that receive blood from veins. LV and RV refer to these two cavities, or ventricles.

The synthetic material Dacron was used to graft the artificial heart to existing arteries in the body.

Below: A girl with a 'bionic' hand. She has an artificial hand (her right) powered by the natural electrical impules delivered by her body muscles. The impulses are amplified electronically and fed to motors that power the artificial hand.

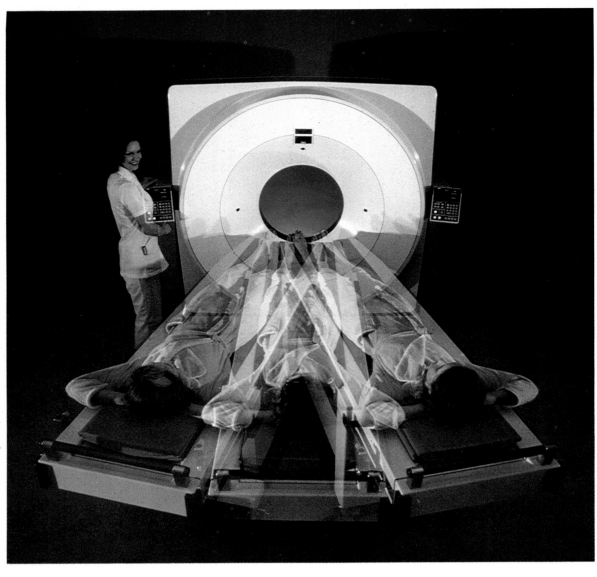

A highly effective alternative to antibiotics is vaccines, for they help the body to build up its own natural defences to disease. The vaccination campaign against smallpox is one of the most notable successes of modern medicine. Since the 1950s, a sustained worldwide effort has entirely wiped out this killer.

One of the biggest achievements of the future promises to be the development of an anti-malaria vaccine. Malaria, one of the six main diseases in the world, kills a million people a year in Africa alone. The search for a vaccine is gathering pace, with some experimental types already being tried out on monkeys. This vaccine will be a custom-built drug designed to do a specific biochemical job. There are many strains of malaria, so it may well be that a whole battery of anti-malaria vaccines will be developed to combat all of them.

Tailor-made Drugs
Some people are fortunate and stay healthy for most of their lives; others fall ill when parts of their bodies start to break down and fail. Sometimes the delicate chemical balance of the body is upset. For example, diabetes develops when the hormone

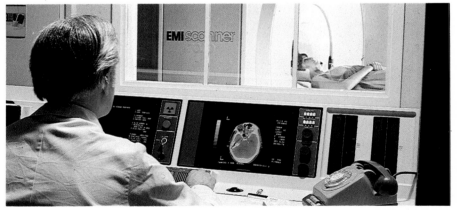

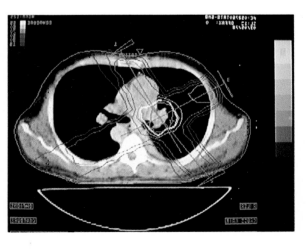

Left: A typical scan of a body slice taken across the chest cavity. Clearly evident are the spine and rib cage.

26

insulin is no longer produced in sufficient quantities.

Replacement hormones were first obtained from natural sources. Insulin, for instance, was taken from the pancreas of a sheep. But these sources could not provide sufficient quantities so scientists had to find ways of making them artificially. They analyzed the hormones to discover their chemical make-up and then set about building a synthetic version.

Some drugs are replicas of natural products. Others have been tailor-made to deal with a specific malfunction and are not found in nature. The drug cimetidine, used to treat peptic ulcers, is one of the first to have been custom-made in this way. Scientists knew what they were looking for when they started. It took twelve years to come up with the answer. But since 1976 new hope exists for the millions of people throughout the world who suffer from peptic ulcers.

In the years to come, more and more tailor-made drugs will be produced to join the fight to save lives.

Microsurgery

Some of the greatest advances are taking place in surgery. Microsurgery has become so sophisticated that severed limbs can be re-joined and cut nerves re-linked. Scalpels no bigger than a pin, and needles as fine as an eye-lash will soon be used in brain surgery to re-route blood vessels that are blocked and could cause fatal strokes.

In conventional surgery, laser scalpels are being improved all the time. They cut very precisely and also cauterize the wound as they go so that bleeding is greatly reduced.

Genetic engineering

In the future an entirely different approach to medicine will arise out of the revolutionary new field of genetic engineering. Scientists have found ways of identifying and isolating the genes in DNA, the molecule that controls the activity of cells and passes on genetic information from one generation to the next.

DNA strands can be broken into fragments containing particular genes. These can be inserted into other DNA molecules to make them behave differently. This technique has already led to hormones being made by parts of the body never designed to do this at all.

In the years ahead, it should be possible for genetic engineers to remove the genes that cause hereditary diseases and psychological disorders from human DNA. It will also be possible to implant genes that reinforce the body's defences against bacteria and viruses and which can also slow down the process of ageing.

Above: A chart showing the average life expectancy over the ages of the human male (females tend to live slightly longer). Only in this century could men reasonably expect to reach the age of 60. The 1980 figures refer to Americans. Life expectancy of people in under-developed countries is still low because of poor diet and inadequate medical care.

Right: Some people seem to live very much longer than average, if the available statistics are to be believed. The old man shown here is from Afghanistan and he claims to be 104 years old!

Treatment of skin tumours by lasers is now well advanced. It is less hazardous than radio-therapy and, in some cases, surgery. Lasers are also finding their way into the operating theatre in the form of the laser scalpel, which cauterizes the flesh as it cuts.

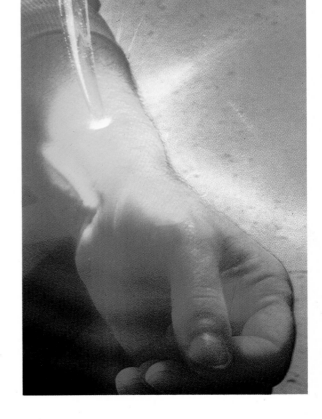

A Shrinking World

One notable feature of 20th century civilization is our mobility. The vehicles that transport us have one thing in common that will affect their role in the world of tomorrow: with the exception of electric locomotives, nearly all are propelled by internal combustion engines using petroleum-based fuels which are becoming increasingly scarce.

For the immediate future, transport engineers are designing engines which burn fuel more efficiently and are looking for alternative engines to take their place in the long term. Unless new, cheap fuel is found, individual private vehicles, which are very wasteful of energy, will be restricted in the future. Instead, publicly owned mass-transit systems of one kind or another will provide in-city and inter-city transportation.

Far-sighted engineers predict that coast-to-coast tube trains travelling at several thousand kilometres an hour may one day be built. Hypersonic air-liners, powered by hydrogen and flying three times as fast as Concorde, will whisk passengers between the continents, while freight will be flown in airships several hundred metres long.

On the Road

The present car petrol engine is very efficient mechanically but not thermally. It can only extract less than one-fifth of the available energy in the petrol. One of several ways of increasing thermal efficiency is by turbo-charging, a method once favoured in racing cars. Extra air is forced into the engine cylinders by a fan driven by a gas turbine in the engine exhaust. Another improvement can be made by charge stratification. The combustion chamber is designed so that a pocket of rich fuel mixture burns before the rest of the mixture, which is weak. Less fuel is consumed and less exhaust pollution is produced.

The diesel engine, too, is much more efficient than the petrol engine. But this advantage is offset by an increase in engine weight, so that the overall saving is reduced. The diesel also used petroleum-based fuel, so in the long term it has all the disadvantages of the petrol engine.

Below: Airships could soon return to the transportation scene after an absence of nearly half a century. They have a number of advantages over aeroplanes. They use power only for propulsion, whereas aeroplanes have to provide power for 'lift' as well. They can take off and land vertically. They are relatively simple to build, and their size is virtually limitless. The use of non-flammable gases such as helium, modern materials and computerized control systems could make the airship a useful vehicle for bulk transportation.

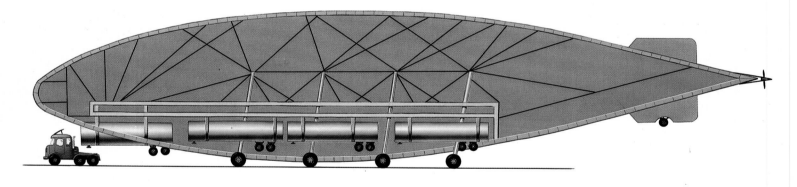

Right: Cross-section of a practical Stirling engine which runs on hot gas. Fuel is burned continuously outside the engine cylinders but heats the working gas inside. The gas is in turn compressed at low temperature and then expanded at high temperature, driving a piston that delivers power.

Above: Simplified diagram of the Lear vapour turbine system which has already been tested in the first steam-turbine-powered car. A pump circulates the fluid, Learium, specially developed for the turbine. The system cools the vapour after spinning the turbine, condensing it to a liquid that can be re-used. The system uses petrol or diesel oil to boil the fluid but emits only a fraction of the pollutants that conventional engines do.

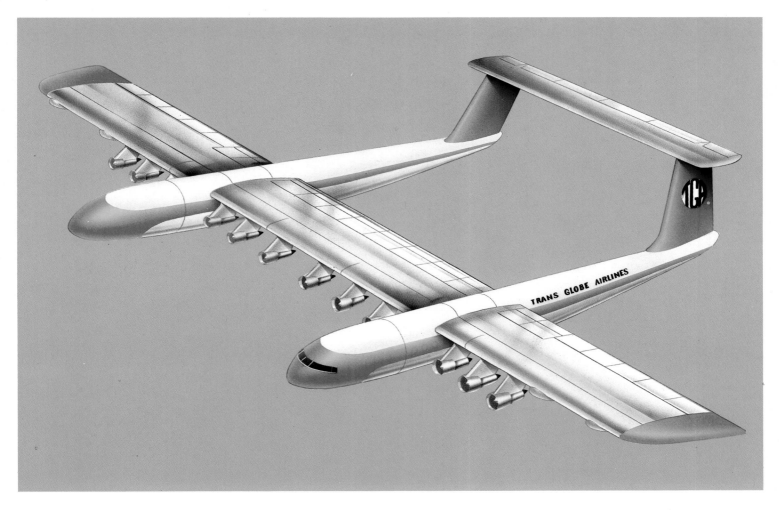

Alternative Engines

With slight modification, the petrol engine can be made to work on hydrogen gas. And it is by using hydrogen that the internal combustion engine can probably survive into the 21st century. One great advantage of a hydrogen engine is that it causes no pollution at all, producing simply water vapour. The hydrogen can be stored in liquid form in a refrigerated tank, but it is better stored in a 'generator' consisting of a compound like metal hydride which absorbs hydrogen readily and releases it when gently heated.

Other alternative engines, while not new, do offer improvements over the conventional petrol engine. One is the Stirling engine, invented by a Scottish clergyman over 150 years ago. It too is a piston engine, but it works differently. The working gas is trapped inside the engine cylinders and is alternately heated and cooled. As its pressure changes, it moves the pistons. The engine burns fuel continuously, quietly and efficiently.

The steam engine was the favoured power source for cars at the beginning of this century. And, in an updated form, it could well be a major source at the century's end. Like the Stirling engine, it burns fuel and therefore causes a little pollution, but only a fraction of that produced by the petrol engine. The early steam cars used water vapour as a working

Above: Giant 12-engined freighters like this could soon be flying through the skies. Its wing span is some 150 metres (490ft).

Below: Research into pollution-free battery-powered cars is intensive, but awaits a breakthrough in battery design. Most promising to date is the zinc-nickel oxide battery which delivers twice as much energy, weight for weight, as the conventional lead-acid battery.

An experimental magnetically levitated (maglev) vehicle travelling at speed. Supported and propelled by magnetism, this kind of vehicle could theoretically approach speeds of 800 kph (500 mph).

fluid, which was afterwards allowed to escape into the atmosphere. This necessitated frequent stops to take on water. The 'steam' car of the future will use the same fluid over and over again, and other liquids will be used instead of water. Also, whereas yesterday's designs were piston engines, tomorrow's will be turbines.

The electric car, popular at the turn of the century, is also staging a comeback. It is very clean and silent and causes no pollution. But it also has drawbacks. The heavy lead-acid batteries that feed power to the electric motor which drives the wheels are heavy and cannot deliver a great deal of energy at once. They also need recharging at frequent intervals. In practical terms this means that the present electric car has poor acceleration, a low top speed and a limited range. For travel in the city these drawbacks do not matter so much, and so electric vehicles will probably be first used on a large scale by city commuters. They could recharge their batteries by plugging into electric points installed in the car parks where they park.

Electronic Aids

More widespread use of electric cars may have to wait for a breakthrough in battery design. One new kind of battery, the sodium/sulphur type, already shows great promise. Alternatively, fuel cells may be used as a power source instead of batteries. The electric car of the future will also be fitted with a means of energy storage such as a flywheel. When going downhill, or when braking, the car will feed energy to the flywheel. This energy will be tapped later to give extra acceleration when required or to recharge the batteries. The use of transistorized and microprocessor

controls will also help give the electric car acceptable performance.

Electronic aids of several kinds will be fitted to future generations of cars, no matter how they are powered. Computers will be fitted to regulate the engine for best performance under all conditions and help diagnose faults. They will be linked in with central traffic-control computers which will feed them constantly updated traffic information. Drivers will be able to call up this information at any time to help them to plan their journey.

To aid safety, the cars will also be fitted with radar and sonar units. These will give drivers information about the proximity of other cars and warn them of the possible dangers of collision. Brakes could also be applied automatically in emergency situations.

However, some people believe that, certainly in cities, the private car will not survive much longer. Travel will be provided instead by a fleet of automatic passenger cars under computer control. They would travel on special tracks or along invisible guide paths following cables laid beneath the streets. Passengers would communicate their travel request to the computer from a terminal at the pick-up point. The computer would then divert the car to its destination.

Flying Trains

Just as the days of the petrol engine are numbered, so are the days of the diesel locomotive, which burns an oil-based fuel. Trains of the future will most probably be all electric. They will not travel on wheels, as now, but fly along the railway track a few centimetres in the air. Their speed will be breath-taking – up to 800 kph (500 mph).

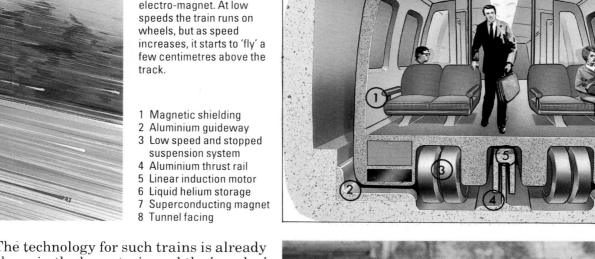

Right: Cross-section of a maglev train. It travels along a track consisting of L-shaped aluminium guide rails on either side. Another rail in the centre forms part of the propulsion unit – a linear induction motor. On board the train is a powerful superconducting electro-magnet. At low speeds the train runs on wheels, but as speed increases, it starts to 'fly' a few centimetres above the track.

1 Magnetic shielding
2 Aluminium guideway
3 Low speed and stopped suspension system
4 Aluminium thrust rail
5 Linear induction motor
6 Liquid helium storage
7 Superconducting magnet
8 Tunnel facing

The technology for such trains is already with us, in the hovertrain and the 'maglev' vehicle. The hovertrain, or tracked air-cushion vehicle, is a development of the hovercraft. It has powerful fans which blow air beneath it to form a cushion, and it glides along on this cushion. Since it is no longer in contact with the track, there is no friction to slow it down, only air resistance.

Since the hovertrain does not use wheels, except at low speed, how is it propelled? Although propellers have been used, as in hovercraft, the method now favoured is the linear motor. This is a modified electric motor which works by magnetic interaction between magnetic coils on the train and a conductor along the track.

The 'maglev' train uses magnetism to lift itself above the track in a different way from the hovertrain. 'Maglev' is short for 'magnetic levitation'. There are several maglev systems, which work on the simple principle of magnetism that two magnets can be made to attract or repel each other. The magnetic interaction between the train and the track can also be made to propel it.

In one maglev system a powerful magnet is installed in the train. When the train moves, it makes the aluminium track beneath it become magnetic and the magnetic repulsion between the on-train magnet and the track causes the train to lift. In an alternative maglev system the levitation of the train is achieved by the controlled attraction of electromagnets. Magnetic levitation features in an even more long-distance transport scheme, the high-speed underground railway, tube or subway. Underground railways are already spreading to more and more cities, helping to beat the increasing traffic

Above: One conception of the car of the future. It is wedge-shaped and is severely streamlined to reduce power-absorbing air resistance. Note the roof-mounted aerofoil to improve the air flow.

Left: Devices that alert drivers to traffic conditions ahead are already at an advanced stage. Up-to-date traffic information is fed into a computer which passes it to a unit in the car via inductive loops in the road surface. A display tells the driver what his maximum speed should be and if he should turn off to avoid any hazard.

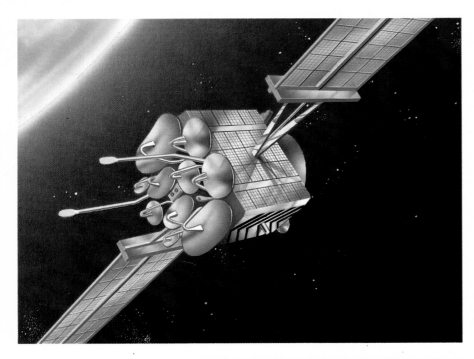

Above: More powerful communications satellites would make it possible to relay intercontinental television broadcasts directly to domestic aerials without the need for expensive ground stations as at present. They could be launched by the space shuttle.

Right: The copper wires now used to carry telephone and telegraph signals for long distances will soon be replaced with optical fibres. These will carry signals in the form of laser pulses.

Below: The aerial display of a satellite communications ground station.

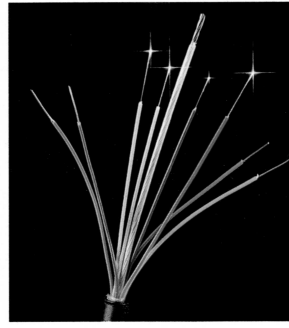

congestion in the streets. But the maglev 'tubes' will be something different. Passengers will travel in sealed cylindrical carriages in evacuated tunnels at speeds in excess of 450 kph (280 mph). It may even be possible, some day, that magnetic levitating trains will travel at the speed of sound, roughly 1223 kph (760 mph).

Telecommunications

As new means of transportation come into use the world seems to grow progressively smaller. A similar thing happens with new means of communication. When news could travel only by runner, horse or ship, communication was slow and the world seemed very large indeed. But in turn the telegraph, the telephone and finally the radio changed all that. Today by means of the telephone we can communicate instantly with people on the other side of the globe. The connection is made through wire and microwave radio links, perhaps via a communications satellite.

Communications satellites have, over the last decade, ushered in an era of more reliable long-distance communications. They are launched into stationary orbit some 35 900 km (22 300 miles) above the Equator over the Atlantic, Pacific and Indian Oceans. In those locations they are able to relay signals all around the world. In the future larger and larger satellites will be built to cope with more and more intercontinental communications. They will be lifted into space by the space shuttle.

The satellites have only a limited life span, however, and have to be replaced every few years. The 'dead' satellites then gradually drift off station, becoming space junk. If they start interfering with other working satellites, they may have to be destroyed by 'hunter-killer' satellites armed with energetic laser or particle beams.

Eventually, when space engineering is well advanced, massive aerial arrays several square kilometres in area could be built in stationary orbit. They would make possible the wrist radio-telephone. This would be a unit similar in size to the digital watch with a built-in microphone/loud-speaker, push buttons for dialling numbers and pop-out aerials. With this device, it would be possible to communicate instantly with anyone in the world who has a similar unit.

Right: An artist's impression of a 'hunter-killer' satellite armed with a laser beam. Satellites of this type may be used in future to destroy useless and dangerous space junk.

Energy

Perhaps the biggest single problem the world has to solve in the future is that of the energy crisis. As the population increases and living standards improve, so does the demand for energy. The trouble is that at present nearly 97 per cent of the energy consumed in the world comes from oil, coal and natural gas. These are fossil fuels, so called because they are the remains of once living things which have fossilized over millions of years. Coal is the remains of gigantic tree ferns; oil and natural gas are products of minute algae and other organisms that teemed in the tropical seas that once covered the Earth.

It has taken many geological ages for the fossil fuels to form. They are being removed at an alarming rate and once they have gone they cannot be replaced. Every day two million tonnes of coal are mined in the United States alone, while in the case of oil, nearly 50 million barrels a day are produced and consumed worldwide (1 barrel = 159 litres or 35 imperial gallons).

New Sources

Known reserves of oil, the most important energy source, indicate that the world will run out of this fuel within thirty years unless consumption is curbed or vast new oilfields are found. The massive increase in the price of oil in the United States during the 1970s, from $2 a barrel at the beginning of the decade to over $25 at the end, reflects the impending scarcity. In their search for new oil supplies, prospectors are looking particularly to the continental shelves, like the North Sea, but are having to develop new technologies to cope with the conditions they find there. North Sea oil development is a case in point.

As the oil gets more and more expensive, hitherto uneconomic sources of oil will be tapped. These include tar sands and oil shales particularly. In the United States there are massive deposits of oil shales in Utah, Wyoming and Colorado. They contain the equivalent of forty times the present American oil reserves. In Canada, the vast Athabasca tar sands contain more oil than exists in the whole of Asia. If these uneconomic resources are used, oil could last for a few more decades.

While the days of oil are all but numbered, those of coal are not. The world has sufficient reserves of coal to last for up to two centuries, perhaps longer. It will switch back to coal in a big way over the next few decades, allowing a breathing space to develop the alternative sources needed next century. Not only will coal be increasingly burned in power stations to

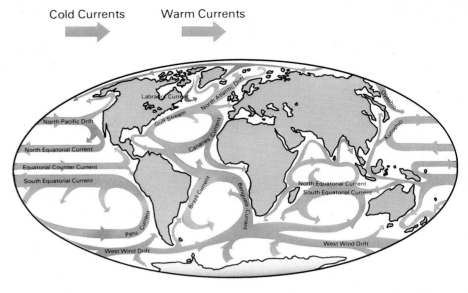

Cold Currents   Warm Currents

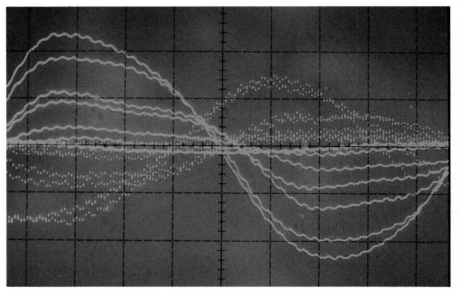

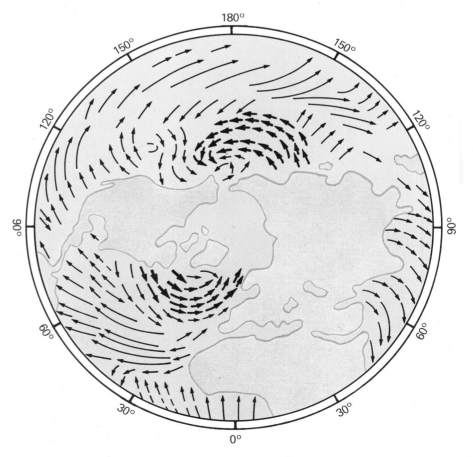

Left (top): A world map of surface currents shows that they tend to flow clockwise around the oceans north of the Equator and anticlockwise south of it. These currents are a natural source of power that could be tapped to provide energy in the future.

Left: An oscilloscope image of the rise and fall of the waves which represents another constantly renewable source of energy.

Bottom left: Diagram showing the prevailing winds in the northern hemisphere in winter. Together with the rotation of the Earth, they cause the constant circulation of the ocean currents. Alone, they represent a large potential power source.

Below: Giant 'ducks' arranged in rows the size of supertankers could convert wave motion to electrical energy. This is one of several schemes to use wave energy that could help ease the current energy problem in the future.

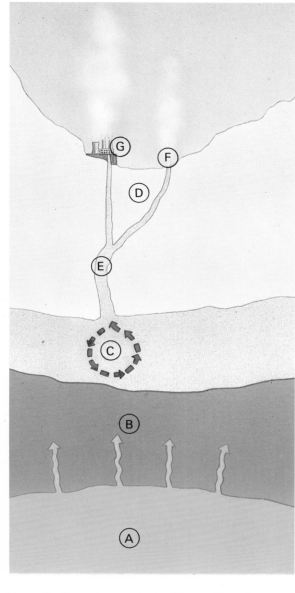

Above: Geothermal power plants utilize heat from the Earth's interior. Heat from molten magma (A) is conducted by solid rocks (B) to a porous rock layer (C) containing water. The water is heated into steam and escapes through fissures (E) in otherwise solid rock (D). The steam escapes as a geyser (F) but can be harnessed at a power plant (G).
Geothermal plants already exist in New Zealand, Italy, Japan, Russia, Mexico, Iceland and the United States.

produce electricity, it will also be converted into synthetic oil.

Germany developed synthetic oil-making plants during World War I when its oil supplies were cut off. By 1980 some countries, notably South Africa, had begun to produce synthetic oil in quantity. In the oil-forming process, coal is turned into gas by treatment with oxygen and steam. It can then be transformed into oil using a chemical catalyst. Other valuable chemicals can be produced as by-products.

The old-fashioned gasworks will also make a comeback in regions with plentiful coal deposits, and coal gas (town gas) will take over when the natural gas, at present being used, runs out. The coal tar produced during this process is a source of valuable organic chemicals, at present extracted from petroleum. Among other fuels that will be used until new technologies are fully developed are alcohol and hydrogen. In the Mid-West United States alcohol, brewed cheaply from corn, is already being added to petrol to eke out supplies, the mixture being called gasohol. Hydrogen, the lightest of all gases, also has great potential: not only does it have very high heating value, it is also non-polluting, forming only water vapour when it burns. Hydrogen can be produced by simple industrial processes and is already available in quantity as a by-product from, for example, oil refining.

Renewable Resources

However much we eke out the remaining supplies of fossil fuels, they will eventually run out. For a long-term solution to the energy problem we must look to renewable energy resources. We find these in the wind, the ocean waves and the Sun. As long as the Earth exists in its present form, as a water-covered planet with an atmosphere, orbiting the Sun, then there will be wind, waves and sunshine; and as long as there is a Moon, there will also be tides in the oceans, which represent another energy source able to be tapped.

There is a further source on our planet geothermal energy. This is the heat locked in the rocks deep down in the Earth's crust. Deep inside the crust, temperatures of over 2000°C (3632°F) may be found. Though the heat gradually leaks away up to the surface, it is continually being replaced by the heat generated by the decay of radioactive elements, such as uranium, thorium and potassium.

We see evidence of geothermal heat in the geysers that exist in many regions of the world, such as Iceland, New Zealand, California and Wyoming. Geysers occur where water percolates through hot spots in the rocks and is boiled to form steam. The steam forces jets of water to the

surface. In some geyser fields this geothermal energy is already being tapped. The steam is piped directly to conventional steam turbines to spin electricity generators. The best places to tap geothermal energy are the regions of the world where earthquakes occur. In these locations the hot rocks lie much closer to the surface.

Wind and Water

No-one who has witnessed the destruction caused by raging flood waters, hurricanes, cyclones and tidal waves (tsunamis) needs reminding of the power locked up in the elements. This power derives ultimately from the Sun and is at present simply going to waste. Our energy-hungry world cannot afford to let this happen and must utilize as much energy from the elements as it can, as soon as possible.

The small wind turbine is used in rural areas mainly for pumping water, for irrigation and for providing water for cattle. Only occasionally is it used for generating electricity at isolated farms. But the new wind turbines now being built are much bigger and are specifically designed to generate electricity. By 1980 the world's most powerful wind generator, located at Boone, North Carolina, had an output of 2 megawatts.

An even more novel wind machine, known as the Darrieus, is also coming into use. It has curved, flexible blades of aerofoil cross-section (like an aeroplane wing) which rotate on a vertical axis. It looks rather like an egg-beater and it readily accepts wind from any direction.

Wind generators, however, have several drawbacks which restrict their use. For example, there are relatively few sites worldwide where the wind blows steadily enough to merit building such machines. Since even at these sites periods of calm frequently occur, wind machines will never be primary energy sources but will be used in conjunction with others. They will, for instance, be integrated into hydro-electric systems. When they are working and the demand for power is high, they will feed electricity into the national grid. When the demand for power is low, they will feed electricity to the turbines used to pump water back to the high reservoir. This form of energy storage (pumped storage) is already practised with many hydro-electric schemes.

The Rhythm of the Oceans

Another power producer is likely to be located offshore in the next decade, extracting energy from waves. The rhythmic up-and-down motion of the waves, caused mainly by the wind, represents a huge potential source of

A possible power scheme (left) uses a massive underwater turbine with a rotor hundreds of meters in diameter. The rotor has to be that large to extract the low-grade energy available and a large mass flow is required to make energy extraction worthwhile.

A prime target for current-energy projects would be the Gulf Stream (called the Florida Current in the United States).

Left: The giant concave mirror of the world's first successful solar furnace towers above the village of Odeillo in the French Pyrenees. In the furnace, placed at the focus of the paraboloid mirror, temperatures of nearly 4000°C (0000F) can be reached.

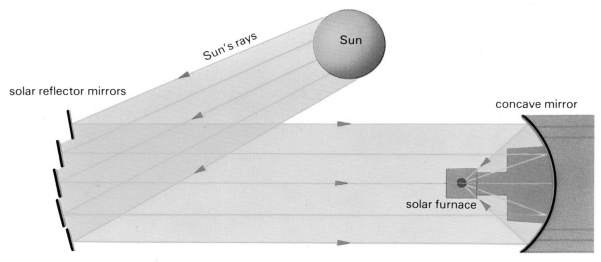

Sun's rays

Sun

solar reflector mirrors

concave mirror

solar furnace

Left: Diagram of the Odeillo solar furnace. Banks of mirrors (heliostats) are lined up on a hillside in front of the concave collector and reflect sunlight upon it. There are 63 heliostats in all, each consisting of 180 separate facets. They are steered as the Sun moves by remote control to keep the sunlight focused on the collector.

energy. As with many natural energy sources, the trouble with wave power is that it is diffused thinly over a vast area. But scientists have come up with devices which make wave power feasible.

The best known of these is called Salter's ducks after their inventor, and consists of a long line of vanes pivoting on a common spine, which head lengthwise into the waves. They each contain an electrical generator which turns as it nods up and down. A full-scale 'duck' generating station will consist of a string of vanes up to 1 kilometre (0.6 miles) long, each vane being something like 15 metres (50 ft) in diameter. The duck will have a power output of up to 30 megawatts.

The ocean currents are another source of power waiting to be tapped. Year in, year out, massive bodies of water move endlessly through the oceans along the same path. They move as they do mainly because of the prevailing winds and the

Coriolis forces – those set up by the rotation of the Earth. In the Atlantic Ocean, for example, there are two great current systems, the Gulf Stream in the North and the Brazil Current in the South. Both are likely candidates for current power schemes.

The Gulf Stream, for example, represents a massive movement of water up to 60 km (40 miles) wide and 600 metres (2000 ft) deep. Again, the trouble is that the movement is relatively slow – about 4 knots (8 kph, 5 mph). So machines of large dimensions will be needed to extract sufficient energy from it. Giant under-water turbines seem to be the best solution, though other schemes have been proposed, including one involving an endless belt of alternately opening and collapsing parachutes.

The other ocean movement that is never-ending is the twice daily rise and fall of the tides. At some locations in the world,

Right: An imaginative scheme for harnessing solar energy indirectly. It is a floating thermal power station and it exploits the temperature difference between tropical surface, which has soaked up the Sun's heat, and the water in the ocean depths.

The engine would work rather like a refrigerator in reverse. An easily vaporized liquid such as ammonia would be alternatively evaporated by the surface water and condensed by cold water from the depths. The circulating vapour would drive power turbines.

The main generating plant would be located near the surface, but the cold-water inlet pipe would plummet to a depth of 500 metres (1600ft) or more.

crew access

ammonia storage

warm water in

evaporator

warm v

pumps

condenser

cold water out

mooring line

cold water in

the tidal range is as high as 15 metres (50 ft), but lower tidal variations can be harnessed. There are perhaps only twenty sites throughout the world where tidal power will be worth extracting with existing technology, and by 1980 only two of these had been developed. One is at the Rance Estuary in France. The plant there has been operating successfully since 1966. Another, much smaller experimental scheme, operates on the White Sea in Russia.

Of the other potential sites two are almost certain to be developed in the years to come. One is in the Bay of Fundy in North America, which has the largest tidal range of all, and the other is the Severn estuary in England. A power scheme in the Severn could provide as much as 6 per cent of Britain's electrical power.

Ocean Thermal Power
There is yet another massive reservoir of energy in the oceans, the energy absorbed from the Sun. As the Sun beats relentlessly down on the surface waters, it heats them to temperatures as high as 30°C (86°F). The deep ocean waters, however, remain much cooler, often as low as 5°C (40°F). There is a significant temperature difference, which can be utilized to power a heat engine. Schemes designed to do this are called OTEC (ocean thermal energy conversion).

Several OTEC schemes have been put forward, which work on essentially similar principles, but vary in design. Basically they are huge floating structures with cold water intake pipes plummeting 500 metres (1600 ft) beneath the surface. They work on similar principles to the refrigerator, continually evaporating and condensing a liquid, such as liquid ammonia. The liquid is evaporated by heat from the hot surface waters, and the vapour is then condensed as it is cooled by the cold water from the deeps. The circulation of the liquid/vapour is used to drive turbo-generators to make electricity. Some detailed designs of 100-megawatt units have already been drawn up and they could be operational before the turn of the century.

Sun Power
The Sun pours onto the Earth 20 000 times more energy than we need at present. The schemes outlined so far would use some of this energy indirectly, but it is also possible to tap solar energy directly. The problem is that it is thinly distributed. In mid-latitudes only about one kilowatt of energy (enough to power a one-bar electric fire) falls on every square metre. Domestically we can use some of this for heating hot water, for space heating in winter, and for running air-conditioning units in the summer (see page 12).

The so-called flat-plate collectors used for domestic solar heating are not suitable for power generation on a large scale. For solar energy on a large scale the sunshine must be concentrated. This is done on a small scale by a magnifying glass, which concentrates all the sunlight falling on the glass to a tiny spot at the focus. There the heat is intense enough to set things alight. In practical schemes for large-scale power generation, the sunshine is concentrated by mirrors rather than lenses.

The first major installation built to use solar energy in this way was the solar furnace at Odeillo in France. Sixty three movable flat mirrors, or heliostats, each with a surface area of 13 square metres (140 square feet) reflected sunlight onto a giant parabolic reflector. This concentrated the sunshine into a searing beam inside a chamber at the focus, where temperatures of 3500°C (6400°F) were obtained.

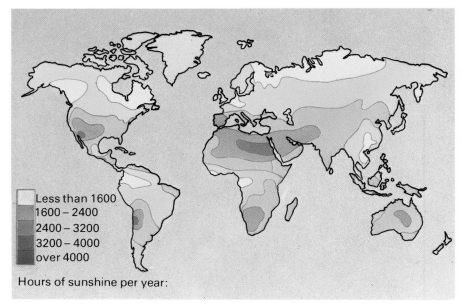

Hours of sunshine per year:

Less than 1600
1600 – 2400
2400 – 3200
3200 – 4000
over 4000

Above: A map showing the amount of sunshine received annually in various parts of the world. Regions with more than 3200 hours (8¾ hours a day) would make good sites for the large-scale development of solar power stations.

Power Towers

Schemes similar to that at Odeillo will soon be employed for power generation in many sunny regions of the world. A typical solar-powered plant consists of a tall tower surrounded by banks of angled mirrors, or heliostats. These mirrors move as the Sun moves so as to direct sunlight continuously onto a receiver at the top of the central tower. Inside the receiver is a boiler in which water, or another liquid, is evaporated and used to drive turbo-generators to produce electricity.

By 1980 schemes had already been tested, notably at Albuquerque, in New Mexico, which had an output of over 5 megawatts. It comprised a 60-metre (200-ft) high tower with banks of 225 reflecting heliostats.

In alternative power generating schemes different methods of harnessing sunlight are used. One uses arrays of curved, para-bolic mirrors which concentrate the sun-light on a fluid-filled tube located at the focus. The fluid is piped to a central station and used to drive turbogenerators.

To generate electricity in any appreciable quantity, the solar-power station will have to occupy a vast area. The hot desert regions of the world are natural locations for them. They are very sparsely populated by humans or animals, so there would be few environmental problems. Indeed there may well be benefits. The solar reflectors would not only afford shade, but also act as dew collectors. This could allow vegetation to grow and support grazing animals. Though the solar stations

Below: Experimental solar power stations are already being built in sunny California and New Mexico in the United States. When fully developed, they could lead to the construction of huge stations like this, capable of generating tens of thousands of kilowatts.

It comprises thousands of flat mirrors (heliostats) which reflect sunlight to a receiver at the top of a central tower. There, water, or another fluid, will be turned into vapour which will be used to drive a turbo-generator and provide electricity.

would often be far from habitation, the power they produce could be transmitted economically by means of microwaves, via relay towers or even space stations.

Satellite Power

Space-age technology will most likely feature in a number of power-generation schemes for the future. In space, satellites and probes obtain their electricity from panels of solar cells. These are wafer-thin crystals of silicon which have an unusual property. When sunlight falls on them, they acquire a slight electrical voltage. When thousands of the 'photo-voltaic' cells are linked together, they produce an appreciable amount of electricity.

Such cells may one day be used in solar power stations on Earth instead of, or as well as, reflector/receiver/generator units. But for a long time they will be too expensive for this. A better scheme is to build the arrays in space where they can be exposed to sunlight for practically all of the time instead of only on clear days on Earth. The electricity produced can then be beamed down to Earth by microwaves.

Even in the perpetual sunshine of space, generation of electricity from solar cells could be too costly, and it is more probable that power satellites will be built first. They consist of a series of linked metal

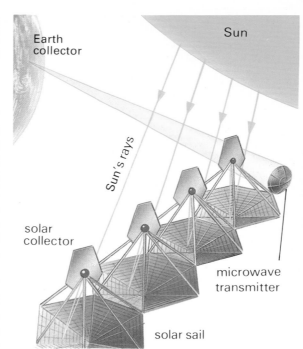

Space satellites already use solar energy on a small scale to provide electricity for their instruments. But in the future satellites may be used to harness solar power for use on Earth. Massive satellites many kilometres across will be required to collect enough energy. They may consist of arrays of solar cells, which convert solar energy directly into electricity, or they may take the form of umbrella-like reflectors. These concentrate sunlight onto receivers in which a fluid is turned into vapour to drive turbo-generators. The electricity produced could be beamed down to Earth in the form of microwaves (see diagram).

Left: The antenna of a solar power satellite ground station, which will collect the microwave energy beamed down to it from space. It will consist of a metal mesh and measure up to 13km (8 miles) across. Land underneath it could still be used for farming.

At the ground station the microwaves will be converted back into electricity and fed into the local grid. Power transmission from the satellite will be continuous except for brief intervals at certain times of the year when it passes through the Earth's shadow.

dishes, which serve as mirrors to reflect sunlight onto absorbers (receivers) located above them. The absorbers contain a working fluid which operates the turbo-generators producing the electricity. The excess heat is disposed of by means of radiators, escaping into the deathly cold of space.

The power generated is routed to a large antenna array, where it is converted into microwaves (very high-frequency waves) and transmitted as a beam to Earth. The solar satellite would be located in an orbit 35 900 km (22 300 miles) above the Earth, over the Equator. In this orbit it would travel once around the Earth every 24 hours, and so remain fixed in the sky relative to the Earth. Its antenna can thus be permanently 'locked' to a ground station, where the microwave energy is received and converted into electricity once again.

The size of a solar power satellite would be enormous. For an output of 10 000 megawatts, reflectors several kilometres across are required, which involve some 100 000 tonnes of construction materials. Building power satellites will undoubtedly be a colossal task, but one that could be

vital by the early years of the 21st century. It offers one of the two best long-term solutions to the world's energy problem. The other solution lies in using the energy that is bound up in the atom.

Power from the Atom

We are already harnessing the power of the atom on quite a large scale, in nuclear reactors. There are about 200 reactors in operation throughout the world, particularly in the United States and Britain, where nuclear power generation was pioneered. Both countries generate over one-eighth of their electricity from nuclear plants. The cost of 'nuclear' electricity is now thought to be lower than 'conventional' electricity obtained from power plants burning fossil fuels.

However, existing types of nuclear plants will not take us very far into the 21st century. They do not consume their nuclear fuel as efficiently as they might, and a new type of reactor will soon replace them, which actually 'breeds' more fuel than it consumes! In its turn the breeder reactor will be replaced by a nuclear reactor working on a totally different principle – fusion rather than fission. It is on fusion reactors that our future energy supplies largely depend.

Fission Reactors

The present generation of nuclear reactors work because heat is given out when atoms of uranium are made to split. The splitting process is called fission. Fission of the uranium atom, or rather its nucleus, occurs when it is bombarded by atomic particles called neutrons. In the fission process, other neutrons are produced which can go on to split other uranium atoms. So a kind of chain reaction takes place.

Uncontrolled, the chain reaction can lead to a catastrophic explosion, as in the atomic bomb. But in a nuclear reactor, the reaction is kept safely under control. It is allowed to proceed just fast enough to produce a suitable heat output. A coolant circulating through the reactor removes this heat, which is then used to raise steam in a boiler. The steam then powers conventional steam turbogenerators, which produce electricity.

Breeder Reactors

Uranium (U) exists in two main forms, or isotopes, U-238 and U-235, and it is only the U-235 which can be split. The uranium fuel used in present reactors contains only a small percentage of U-235. When this is used up, the remainder of the uranium (U-238) has to be discarded, for it cannot undergo fission. In breeder reactors, however, things will improve. Experimental breeder reactors in Britain and

Below: Atoms are so small that if an atom were the size of your little finger nail, then your hand would be large enough to grasp the Earth!

France are already proving their superiority in many respects.

The breeder reactor uses a highly enriched uranium fuel containing more U-235 than usual. This fuel can be split readily by fast neutrons, unlike the fuel in present reactors, which can only be split by slow neutrons. The fast neutrons not only affect U-235, they also affect U-238, changing it into an isotope of plutonium (Pu-239). The advantage of this process is that the plutonium can be used as fuel for the reactor. So in this type of reactor the enriched fuel is surrounded by a blanket of U-238, which is periodically removed to extract the plutonium.

Danger: Radiation!

The great benefits of nuclear fission power, however, are attended by great drawbacks. Uranium is unlike most chemical elements in that it is unstable. Its atoms are continually breaking down, giving off high-speed particles and radiation. We say

Britain and France have had most experience in breeder-reactor operation. Britain has been producing electricity from its Prototype Fast Reactor (right) at Dounreay for some years, while France will soon put into operation the first large-scale plant at Creys-Malville, seen below under construction.

Below: A fusion reaction is the synthesis of a heavy atom from two light nucleii with a simultaneous release of energy. The diagram shows the fusion of a deuterium nucleus with a tritium nucleus, forming a helium nucleus and one neutron. The quantity of energy produced per gramme of fuel is equal to that released from the combustion of more than 10 000 litres of petrol.

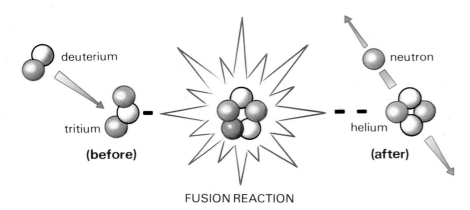

deuterium
tritium
(before)
neutron
helium
(after)

FUSION REACTION

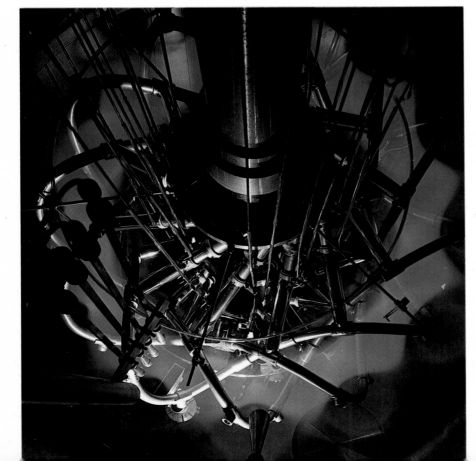

it is radioactive. The nuclear fission process, as well as releasing abundant energy, releases streams of radiation. The spent fuel from nuclear reactors remains radioactive for thousands of years.

Radioactive materials give out three main kinds of radiation, called alpha-rays, beta-rays and gamma-rays. All these rays, particularly the last, are dangerous to living things, plants and animals alike. They are very penetrating, and in large enough doses can damage or kill living tissue. Even in smaller doses they can do harm, though it might not be immediately evident. For radiation can effect the genes of living things, causing mutations, or changes, to occur in subsequent generations. So the offspring of parents exposed to radiation may have characteristics, good or

Left: Gaseous plasma glows purple in an experiment that could make the heavy hydrogen in seawater a vital source of energy produced by nuclear fusion. If the superheated plasma touched the sides of its container these would melt. Experimental devices like the one shown use magnets to make sure this cannot happen.

bad, which neither of the parents possesses.

Strict precautions are taken in nuclear establishments to contain the hazard of radiation. Nuclear reactors are surrounded by thick shielding, consisting of several metres of concrete. Radioactive materials are always kept in lead-lined containers and handled by remote-control devices. But accidents and leaks have occurred.

'Meltdown'

Some people fear that nuclear reactors will get out of control and explode like an atomic bomb. There is virtually no chance of this happening because so many failsafe devices are built into the reactor systems. The greatest danger is the possibility of a 'meltdown', a situation in which the reactor overheats and the core melts. Unless it is stopped molten radioactive material would then escape. A meltdown almost occurred at a nuclear plant at Three Mile Island, Pennsylvania, in 1979, which attracted a great deal of attention throughout the world and called into question the wisdom of 'going nuclear' in a big way. The disposal of radioactive wastes from reactors also poses a long-term environmental problem (see page 65).

The Promise of Fusion

The world can still 'go nuclear', however, without the hazards associated with uranium, plutonium and nuclear fission. It can do so by exploiting another type of nuclear reaction, known as fusion. Nuclear fusion is a process in which different types of hydrogen atoms are made to join together, or fuse. When this happens, huge amounts of energy are released. The process contrasts with fission, in which energy is released when heavy atoms are made to split.

Nuclear fusion is the process that gives the Sun and stars their energy. In the interior of stars, atoms of hydrogen fuse together to form helium atoms. It is this process which scientists seek to imitate, in fusion experiments on Earth. They have already achieved such fusion, but in an uncontrolled way, in the devastating hydrogen bomb. The problem is to achieve fusion in a controlled way and make a nuclear fusion reactor.

To create suitable conditions for fusion to occur is difficult on Earth. Temperatures of several million degrees are required before the reaction will occur. At such temperatures, matter exists as a plasma in

Below: Devices like this are known as Tokamaks. They are a means of producing and confining beams of searing hot plasma at temperatures of millions of degrees so that nuclear fusion can occur. Tokamaks consume vast quantities of electricity to produce and heat up the plasma and to energize the powerful electromagnets required to confine it.

1 Magnetic field coils

2 Magnetic field coils

3 Core

4 Blanket module

5 Cooling ducts

6 Duct joints

7 Shield structure and vacuum wall

8 Shield door

9 Shield cooling

10 Shield support

11 Servicing floor

12 Injector, refuel and control access

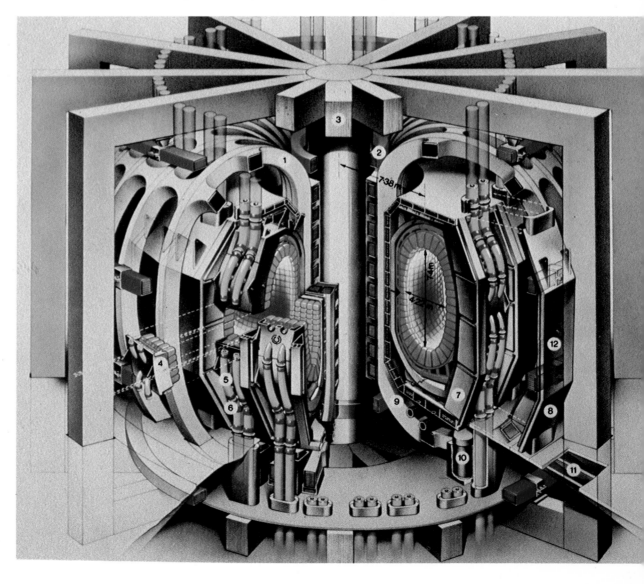

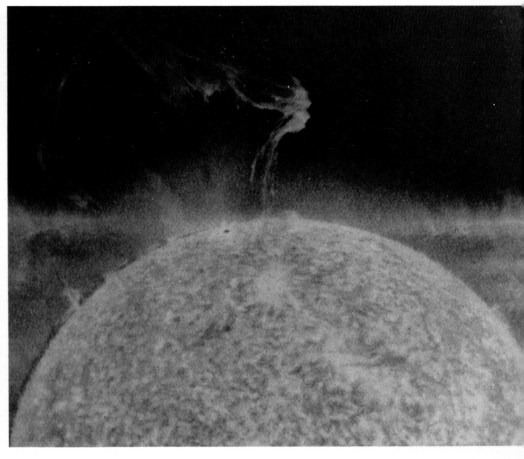

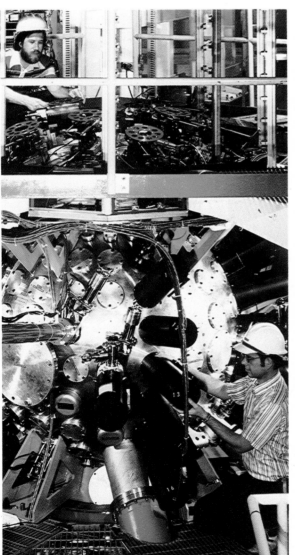

which the atoms are stripped of their electrons. To achieve fusion, the hydrogen must be converted into a very high temperature plasma long enough for the reaction to take place. And, of course, the plasma must somehow be contained. Many fusion researchers use electromagnetic methods to produce and contain plasma. They work with huge machines such as tokomaks, which hold the plasma in a torus, or doughnut-shaped cavity.

Lasers

Other researchers plan to achieve fusion in another way, by using powerful laser beams. Research is most advanced in the United States, using one of the most powerful lasers in the world, known as Shiva. In principle, laser fusion works like this. The laser light is split up into several beams which are then used to bombard a tiny pellet of heavy hydrogen (deuterium and tritium) from all directions. The laser pulse causes the pellet to compress so explosively that it reaches fusion temperature. In a working reactor, the fusion chamber would be surrounded by a bath of liquid lithium, which would extract the heat. This would then be used to raise steam for turbo-generators in the normal way.

When nuclear fusion reactors come into use, maybe as early as the 1990s, the world's energy crisis will begin to ease. Their fuel, heavy hydrogen, can be readily obtained from the vast oceans that cover more than two-thirds of our planet.

Above: Activity on the surface of the Sun, which shines by means of nuclear fusion. In its 15 000 000°C interior, hydrogen fuses into helium with the release of enormous energy.

If we can imitate the process on Earth, we can look forward to a future free from energy worries.

While some researchers experiment with Tokamaks (opposite), others adopt a different approach, using lasers to bring about fusion.
The Lawrence Livermore Laboratory in California has built the world's most powerful laser, Shiva, and is using it to bombard tiny pellets of heavy hydrogen. The energy of bombardment is so great that the pellet implodes into plasma.
The photographs (left) show a pellet centralized in the target chamber on the end of the positioner (top), and technicians working in the target area (bottom).

Raw Materials

The world is running short not only of materials that produce energy but also of many metals and other raw material. The main materials used today are iron and steel which is made from iron. But in addition to iron, we use for one purpose or another the majority of the other metals that exist in the Earth's crust. Aluminium, copper, nickel, chromium, manganese, uranium, platinum, gold, silver and lead are all important.

Diminishing Supplies
With few exceptions, the metals are obtained from the Earth's crust in the form of a mineral ore. This then has to be processed in various ways to obtain the metal. To satisfy our demands for metals, unbelievable quantities of minerals must be mined each year. Some 300 million tonnes of iron ore are mined annually by Russia and the United States alone. Fortunately, the Earth can cope with this rate of production of iron ore because it is found in vast quantities throughout the world. It should last for at least another 300 years. The strong, lightweight metal aluminium exists in great quantities in the Earth, but only in a few locations does a usable ore like bauxite occur. It is estimated that bauxite will be exhausted by about the year 2100. By then methods will undoubtedly have been found to extract alu-

minium from clay, which contains abundant quantities of aluminium minerals.

The situation with copper is much more serious. This metal, so vital to the electrical industry, could be worked out just after the turn of the century if present production rates continue. So could uranium, platinum, gold, silver and lead. The shortage of uranium will be a blow to the nuclear power industry. The lack of platinum will greatly affect industry because it is a vital catalyst in many production processes, for example, in oil refining and in the manufacture of sulphuric acid, often called the 'lifeblood' of industry.

The shortage of gold and silver will also have far-reaching consequences, and not only in industry. Many nations keep much of their wealth in gold bullion. Without silver the photographic industry will go into a decline because silver salts are the essential substances in the light-sensitive emulsion of photographic film.

Beating the Shortage
Geologists, scientists and engineers are now making a concerted effort to ensure a continuing supply of raw materials. First they are stepping up the search for new mineral deposits. Secondly, they are investigating new and better processes for extracting metals and for recycling metals that are at present going to waste. Thirdly,

It has taken millions of years for deposits of minerals to form in the Earth's crust. Mineral formation is still going on but, except on the ocean floor, not at a rate that will affect the mineral shortage in the foreseeable future.

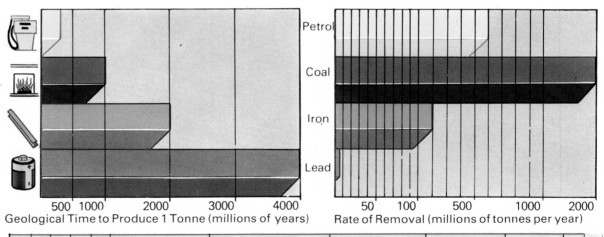

Geological Time to Produce 1 Tonne (millions of years)

Rate of Removal (millions of tonnes per year)

Reserves of our two most important structural metals, iron and aluminium, are vast and will satisfy the demands of the world for centuries. But the position of other metals in common use is grave. Tin, copper, zinc and lead, most widely used in the form of alloys, could run out by the first decade of the 21st century.

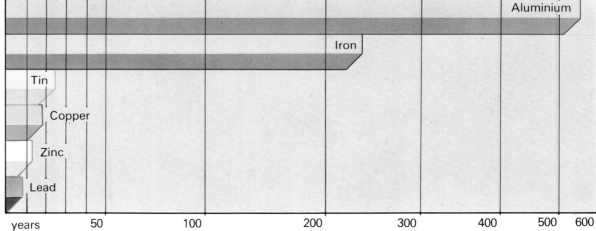

they are looking not only on land, but also in the seas to provide mineral wealth. Fourthly, they are developing alternative materials to take the place of metals. For the more distant future, they suggest we may even start mining the Moon, the asteroids and perhaps other planets.

Prospecting for minerals has become increasingly difficult as obvious deposits run out. Geologists have to use ever more sensitive scientific instruments in their search, from magnetometers and gravity meters to scintillation counters (for radio-active minerals) and seismographs.

Seismic surveying, which involves sending shock waves through the ground, is used particularly to search for oil and natural gas. It can now be done as accurately offshore as it is on land. But the greatest advances in seismic surveying, as with other forms of prospecting, have been brought about by the introduction of computers to analyze the masses of data the geologists acquire. They can even be programmed to produce colour-coded scans on which likely deposits stand out in the rock profile.

Great advances have also been made in satellite prospecting. Thousands of pictures have been taken by the series of Landsat Earth survey satellites from an altitude of several hundred kilometres.

They have yielded a surprising amount of hitherto unknown information about surface rock formations. These satellites view the ground at four different wave-lengths and tend to see things that are normally invisible to the human eye. Also, from their lofty viewpoint they show a much better general picture of formations than is possible otherwise

New Ways of Drilling

Finding a hint of a new deposit is only the beginning. Lengthy drilling operations are then required to find out whether a deposit really exists. In Oklahoma, a hole over 9.5 km (6 miles) deep has been bored to tap natural gas. Drilling holes of such depth is costly, but will become increasingly necessary as deposits run out. Drilling at sea is even more difficult, more expensive and more hazardous. It may be done by fixed drill rigs, semi-submersible rigs or drill ships, depending on the depth of water. The latter can drill in depths of up 400 metres (1300 ft). The technology that has been developed for deep submarine drilling for oil and gas will enable greater exploitation of the seas in the years to come, when permanently staffed undersea work stations will be operated (see page 50).

As well as searching for new mineral deposits, miners are returning to old

This stunning picture reflects the scale of some mining activities. It shows the world's largest excavation – the Bingham Canyon Copper Mine south of Salt Lake City in Utah, USA.

Over 3400 million tonnes of ore have been extracted from the mine since 1906. The excavation covers an area of over 7 square kilometres (nearly 3 square miles) and is over 775 metres (2500ft) deep.

deposits that were once uneconomic to work. In many cases the steep and increasing rise in metal prices now makes this worthwhile. It is not only the mines themselves that are being re-opened. Often the massive 'spoil heaps' containing waste from the old workings can now be profitably processed as well.

Recycling

In the majority of cases the way we use metals does not destroy them. Metal objects (except for those made from precious metals) are usually thrown away when their usefulness ceases. This happens, for example, to old cars, which are dumped on the scrapheap and left to corrode away. Until recently it has been cheaper to dump them than to try to do anything with the metal they contain. But things are changing, and it is becoming economic as well as sensible to recycle, or use again, the raw materials in things like the car.

The amount of metal conserved just by recycling cars would be colossal. Most cars contain between about 500 kg and 1000 kg of metal (1100-2200 lb), and several million cars are scrapped every year. Most of the metal in a car is cast iron and mild steel, but there are also significant amounts of aluminium, copper (in the electrical system), lead (in the batteries) and other relatively scarce constituents. There are of course many other sources of metal scrap which could be recycled, from retired ships, buses and trains to TV sets, washing machines, refrigerators, bicycles, buckets, kitchenware and tin cans. Many of the larger items are at present simply left to rust away, while the smaller items are removed with the rubbish and eventually buried with other household refuse.

Such wastage on a world-wide scale will soon be stopped when governments give greater priority to recycling, and scientists discover better ways of doing it. An example of the ingenious new technology being tried is the supercold treatment of scrap cars to separate the ferrous metals, such as iron and steel, from the non-ferrous, such as aluminium and copper. Treating the car with liquid nitrogen, at a temperture of $-196°C$ ($-325°F$), makes the ferrous metals brittle but has little effect on the non-ferrous. Then the steel in the car body will shatter into small pieces under impact, rather as glass does. It can then be more readily separated from the non-ferrous metals which remain more or less intact.

Mining the Oceans

The oceans cover 71 per cent of the Earth. It has been estimated that they contain and conceal at least as much mineral wealth as was originally on the land before mining

activities began. This wealth is present as chemicals dissolved in the sea-water, as deposits on the sea floor or as deposits in the rock of the continental shelf.

Dissolved chemicals, or salts, make up about 3.5 per cent of sea-water. The most common salts are chlorides, though there are also sulphates, bromides, iodides and fluorides. The most abundant salt by far is sodium chloride, or common salt, followed by magnesium chloride and sodium sulphate. There are many other metals dissolved in the sea besides sodium and magnesium, including calcium, potassium, uranium and gold.

Below: Offshore crude-oil production will increase significantly in the years to come as more and more deposits are found on the continental shelf. Existing technologies will be refined and extended, and underwater complexes like this may be developed. After oil wells have been drilled from floating drilling ships, service modules will be dropped down over them on the seabed so that engineers can supervise the transfer of oil to storage tanks.

drilling rig

supply ship

oil processing

mooring lines

oil stora

wellhead

workshops and laboratories

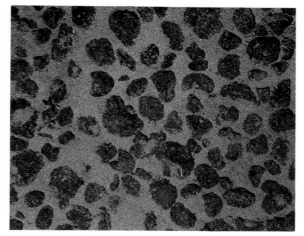

Right: Manganese nodules like this occur in abundance on the seabed in deep oceans. They are a rich source of many vital metals that will soon be in short supply.

storage tanks

tanker

submersible

submersible

entrance hatch

For centuries common salt has been obtained from the seas by allowing sea-water to evaporate from shallow basins, leaving crystals of salt behind. This is still the major source of supply in many countries. Sea-water is also the main source of magnesium, the light-weight metal vital to aerospace construction, and bromine, a widely used industrial chemical. Both elements are obtained by means of electrolysis.

Gold, silver, tin, titanium and uranium all occur in sea-water, but too scantily to make extraction feasible. However, we know that some marine plants and animals can concentrate rare substances. Such *bio-accumulation* produces pearls in oysters and iodine in seaweeds. We may yet find and farm sea organisms capable of concentrating other useful substances. Already, we know oysters build pearls by coating small foreign bodies such as particles of sand with layers of nacre which they make from substances in sea-water. Oysters also accumulate zinc in their body tissues. Other sea cretures concentrate copper, niobium, vanadium – elements scarce in sea-water. One day they may help to satisfy our needs for some rare metals.

Seaweed as Raw Material
Iodine has also long been extracted from sea-water by a rather indirect route. It is extracted from the ash remaining after burning seaweed which somehow concentrates the iodine in its tissues. At present only a small amount of iodine is obtained in this way. But when other deposits run out, seaweed could become the major source. This fits in with schemes to farm seaweed on a large scale for energy production.

Certain seaweeds grow very rapidly and are very efficient at converting sunlight into chemical energy which is released when they are burned. But they are also sources of food. The most likely candidate for seaweed farming is the giant kelp, *Macrocystis pyrifera*. Already farmed in China and Japan, it can grow at a rate of 0.6 metres (2 ft) a day and up to 90 metres (300 ft) long. Eventually, by genetic engineering (page 27), it may be possible to alter seaweed and other marine plants so that we can extract other vital elements from sea-water.

Dredging the Oceans
Valuable ore deposits are also found on the seabed. Offshore seabed mining is already being carried out, for example, for the tin ore called cassiterite. Cassiterite is a heavy mineral which occurs in deposits in stream beds and lakes and also in river estuaries. It is extracted by huge floating dredges, which commonly operate in depths of 30-40 metres (100-130 ft) at distances up to 8 km

Right: Metals in the form of dissolved minerals abound in sea water but are sparsely distributed, and with one vital exception they will probably never be exploited. That exception is magnesium, of which there is some 6 million tons per cubic mile (1.4 tonnes per cubic kilometre) Much of our magnesium is already extracted from sea water. The concentration of other metals in sea water is very much lower, as the table shows.

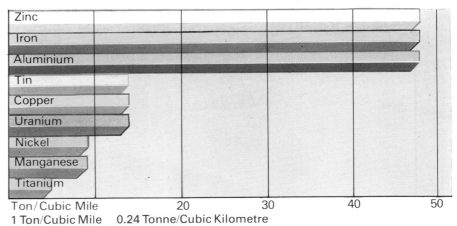

		20	30	40	50
Zinc					
Iron					
Aluminium					
Tin					
Copper					
Uranium					
Nickel					
Manganese					
Titanium					

Ton/Cubic Mile
1 Ton/Cubic Mile   0.24 Tonne/Cubic Kilometre

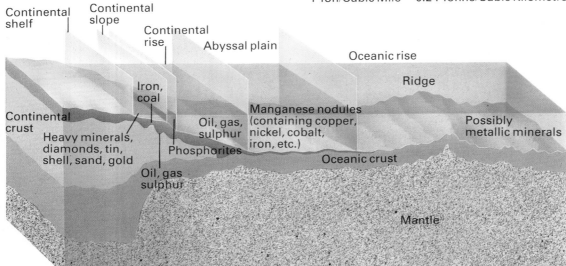

Continental shelf
Continental slope
Continental rise
Abyssal plain
Oceanic rise
Ridge
Continental crust
Iron, coal
Oil, gas, sulphur
Manganese nodules (containing copper, nickel, cobalt, iron, etc.)
Possibly metallic minerals
Heavy minerals, diamonds, tin, shell, sand, gold
Phosphorites
Oil, gas sulphur
Oceanic crust
Mantle

Left: A typical cross-section of the ocean floor, showing where different types of mineral resources are found.

Below: Three methods of extracting manganese nodules from the deep ocean floor. The ship on the left 'vacuums' them off the bottom. The two ships in the middle pull the continuously moving series of dredge buckets that scoop up the nodules. The system on the right relies on remote controlled collectors that shuttle between the ocean floor and the surface platform.

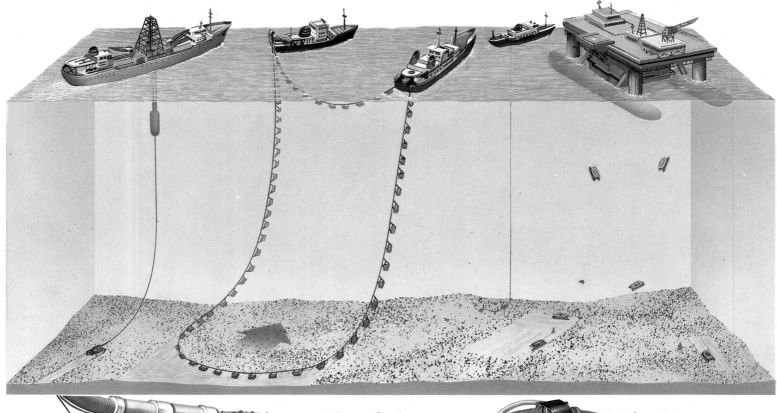

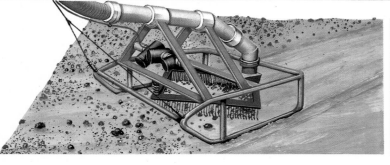

(5 miles) offshore. Undoubtedly there are still offshore seabed deposits to be discovered in shallow seas, where they could be exploited relatively easily.

Some of the most valuable submarine deposits, however, are found on the seabed in the deep ocean. Dredging the deep ocean floor could well prove worthwhile. The main attraction is millions of rounded, metallic lumps scattered on the seabed — especially in the Pacific Ocean. These lumps are called *manganese nodules*, but they also contain cobalt, copper and nickel and other substances whose land deposits are rapidly dwindling.

Geologists believe that the nodules grow from minerals in the water which collect around objects, such as fish teeth, lying on the seabed. The nodules range in size from pebbles to rocks that weigh a tonne. They grow slowly — probably by only 0.1 millimetre in a thousand years. But this is actually faster in total than the rate at which we use some of the metals that they contain.

High Cost

Dredging useful quantities from great depths poses major problems. So does separating the ingredients, whose useful contents vary in amount and are lower than people once believed. By 1980 mass dredging had not started, and it may be years before it can be made to pay. Test dredgings, however, have already recovered nodules from depths up to 5 km (3 miles). The illustration on the left shows methods of deep-sea dredging that could be used. The continuous-bucket and hydraulic systems have already been successfully demonstrated and will be the first to be used commercially. The only real drawback to going ahead with nodule mining is cost, for an investment of some $300 000 000 (£150 000 000) would be required for the mining ship, ore barge and necessary processing plant. And, on the whole, the minerals that can be mined from the sea are unfortunately not the ones which are at present in short supply.

Glass-fibre has been used for many years as reinforcement in plastic composites. Recently, glass-fibres have found application in building construction as re-inforcement in concrete (right). In their search for extra strength or lightness in structures, scientists and engineers will continue to experiment with such composite materials.

Carbon fibres are now widely used for reinforcement in plastic composites. These composites are noted for their lightness, stiffness, strength and resistance to fatigue and wear.

The European 'Tornado' multi-role combat aircraft (MCRA) is one of many advanced jet planes which use carbon-fibre reinforced components.

Golf shafts, fishing rods, tennis raquets and ski poles have also exploited the potential of carbon fibre composites.

Left: Lunar rocks under a microscope. Rare elements such as chromium, titanium and zirconium are found in large amounts in lunar rocks and may provide a useful source in future.

Work and Play

The impending shortage of energy and raw materials are two of the most pressing issues that affect our thinking about the future. But if history is anything to go by we should not worry too much. The chances are that we shall find solutions to these and other problems because we have to, as has happened in the past, particularly in the past two centuries. This period was marked by the accelerating revolution in industry. The breakthrough that sparked off the original Industrial Revolution was the harnessing of a convenient and reliable power source in the steam engine.

Mechanization

There followed the many and various machines that provided industry with the means to increase its productive capacity. The machines also freed workers from a great deal of heavy, tedious work and so saved energy. Such mechanization was initially opposed by the workers, who thought their jobs would be eliminated. But they did not foresee that mechanization would bring about such a demand for manufactured goods that more and more factories, employing more and more people to mind and operate the machines, would be required. Mechanization therefore brought about increased employment of a different kind.

The next significant step in industrial expansion was the development of precision machine tools. These tools were able to produce machine parts with a high degree of accuracy so a machine could be assembled from a set of parts. Before then, every machine was made individually, with parts being tailor-made and assembled by skilled craftsmen. Precision machine tools made manufacturing by mass production possible.

Rise of Robots

Mass production uses relatively unskilled labour to assemble precisely matching components step by step into a finished product. Its other features are an assembly line and moving conveyor. Human labour, however, still provides essential links in the production chain. In the future, people will all but disappear from many assembly lines if their places are taken by suitably programmed robots.

In some car assembly plants robots have already taken the place of workers. Robot welders, for example, spot-weld car bodies with a precision far greater than their human counterparts could consistently achieve. With proper maintenance, they can continue doing so indefinitely without ever tiring, needing refreshment or getting bored as human beings do.

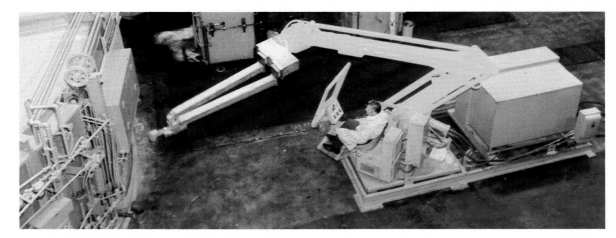

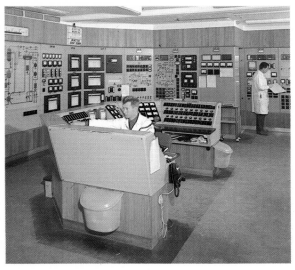

The industrial robot, however, is far removed from the popular notion of a robot. Although it may have 'arms' and 'eyes' of a sort, it is not a human machine or android. The human frame is not suited to many industrial tasks, so robots are purpose-built and take whatever form is most suitable for particular purposes.

Purpose-built robots are still very expensive and can normally only do one job. Research is therefore proceeding on the design of multi-purpose robots which will be able to tackle a variety of tasks. To be effective, such robots need to possess many of the faculties which a human being possesses. Multi-purpose robots will require 'senses' (sensors) and 'limbs' of some kind and the ability to co-ordinate one with the other. Each robot will also require a controlling unit which can be given instructions and act upon them. In other words, a 'brain' would be needed. At present, we have the individual components for such robots. If we need them in the future, we have only to link the components together.

Automation
The industrial robots that already exist are not worked by human operators. They receive their instructions from another machine, a computer. A computer not only operates the individual machines but also co-ordinates the operation of them all, together with the transfer of components between them. The whole system works automatically and is self-correcting. Should any link in the production chain get out of phase, the computer is programmed to adjust the flow of materials or the actions of the machines.

The use of computer-controlled machines is known as automation. It is the next step up from mechanization which brought about a similar revolution in industry two centuries ago.

Automation is particularly suited to chemical processing because the materials being handled can be readily transferred from place to place. In other branches of industry transfer of components can present problems, with the result that some production lines can often only be partly automated.

Control Computer
Oil refining, however, has already been entirely automated. The refinery control computer is first fed information about what is happening in various parts of the refinery at any time. It stores this information in its memory. It is linked to sensors throughout the refinery which tell it what actually *is* happening. The control computer is programmed so that it can compare the actual readings from the sensors (of temperature, pressure, flow rate, and so on) with the ideal readings stored in its memory. If the readings differ, then the computer sends signals to heaters, pumps or valves to switch on or off as necessary to correct the errors. With the computer in charge, refining is self-regulating. The computer takes care of all communications and control within the plant.

Cybernetics
The similarity between communications and control systems in machines and animals has given rise to a branch of science known as cybernetics. Both the control engineer and the biologist study cybernetics. They can compare, for example, the human brain to a machine's 'brain'.

We popularly call the computer an electronic brain. It cannot think for itself and must blindly obey the programme or set of instructions it is given by human beings. Yet, with the help of human intelligence, it can perform prodigious feats. It can control a refinery as we have seen, play chess like a Grand Master, and it can guide a planetary probe hundreds of millions of kilometres through space to achieve a soft landing on other planets.

Speed and Accuracy

The computer can perform such feats partly because of the sheer speed at which it operates. It can carry out hundreds of thousands of accurate arithmetical and logical functions per second. Moreover, it can store, arrange and compare all manner of data which can be represented in digital or number form. In other words, it can help us to solve problems too complex for us to tackle by ourselves. So human intelligence has been extended by the remarkably 'intelligent' machines we have made.

Artificial Intelligence

Some computer experts have suggested that there could be such a thing as 'machine intelligence' or artificial intelligence (AI) and are carrying out studies in this field. There is a growing fear that, as computers become faster and more complex, people will start to lose control of them. Computer operators cannot always understand how and why computers make their decisions, because human beings and computers reason and respond to situations in different ways. Computers are always logical: human beings are sometimes not. Arising from this difference, there have already been near-disastrous consequences at an American nuclear power plant, Three Mile Island in Pennsylvania, and at an early warning missile tracking station. In both cases the control computers sent out alarm signals, but the supervisors could not understand why, which caused confusion and delay before people responded to the signals.

The purpose of AI experiments is to investigate the nature of machine intelligence so that we can benefit from it. Researchers are trying to understand the machine mind so that they can fully appreciate the way in which machines reach decisions. They will need such understanding if they are to remain competently in control in the future when computers are likely to become commonplace in the home and the office, as well as in industry and commerce.

AI researchers also seek to improve methods of communications between operator and computer, an area that has always limited the widespread application

Grains of sand containing the element silicon. An insulator when pure silicon becomes a semi-conductor when traces of other elements are added to it. It is this characteristic of silicon that is close to the thermionic valve and this is why it can effectively replace it.

The first stage in chip processing is to produce large perfect crystals of pure silicon. This is then sliced into the thinnest disc-shaped wafers from which the chips will eventually be cut.

Human ingenuity has reduced each element of electronic circuitry to miniscule proportions. Circuitry is now so complex that computers are used to project any section of it on a screen. A designer using a light pen can then amend design details on the circuit.

56

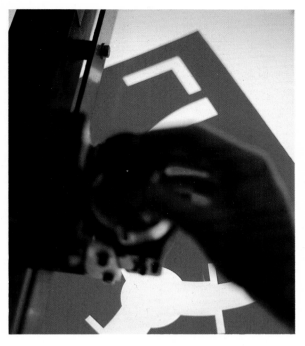

The corrected computer information is used to cut the large scale masters from plastic sheeting for the photo-reduction processes of each layer of the chip. Impurities, or dopants, are diffused into some of the layers of the silicon to produce electrically different regions. There may be as many as a dozen layers, some of which act as insulators, others as electrical connectors and semi-conductors. There may be several hundred chips on each disc-shaped wafer. (see page 59)

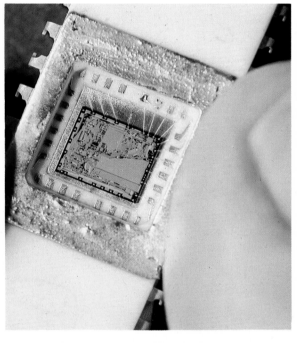

A computer-linked probe next scans the disc for defective circuits and marks any chips that are unusable. A diamond cutter then slices the wafer into individual chips each of which are then mounted on a ceramic base. The finest gold wire connects the chip to tiny pads surrounding it; the pads are linked to pins.

The pins which link the chip to the electrical connecting board is clearly shown here. Each chip is part of a wider network, its functions linked with the functions of other chips on the connecting board. It is astonishing to think that a few chips linked together can have a computing ability equal to that of a room-size computer of only 20 years ago.

of computers. At present, operators and computers communicate haltingly through a computer 'language' such as Fortran and Cobol. Operators first have to translate their instructions into the language; the computer then translates the language into digits so that it can process the instructions. This is a cumbersome method and prone to human error. More natural languages are now being developed, and great advances have been made in direct voice-communication systems. Within the foreseeable future, it is likely that these will be combined so that we can communicate with computers simply by talking.

Computer Hardware

The means of communicating with and programming a computer form part of what is called computer software. The hardware is the physical part of the computer and includes the input, control, memory, arithmetic and output units. The input feeds data into the computer via punched cards, magnetic tape, floppy disc or keyboard. It may also incorporate a video display unit like a TV screen. The memory stores all the required data. The control unit extracts from the memory the operating instructions, or programme, and commands the arithmetic unit to carry out the necessary mathematical operations. The output unit delivers the results of the computation on a video screen, printed sheet, magnetic tape and so on.

The Binary System

A computer works by manipulating numbers, not as decimals but as ones and noughts in the so-called binary number system. In the computer, ones and noughts can be represented by the flow or non-flow of an electric current, so computers consist essentially of banks of on/off switches. The capacity of a computer is usually expressed by the number of binary digits ('bits') it can handle.

The first experimental computer used electro-mechanical switches; the first commercial computers were electronic, using electron valves which were much faster in operation. But to gain sufficient computing power, the computers occupied large rooms because they used up thousands of electron valves and several kilometres of connecting wire. They also required upwards of 20 kilowatts of electrical power.

The Transistor Revolution

In the 1950s the transistor revolution began. Transistors are electronic devices which do the work of electron valves but are many times smaller and have at their centre tiny pieces of silicon. They are also more reliable and require much less power

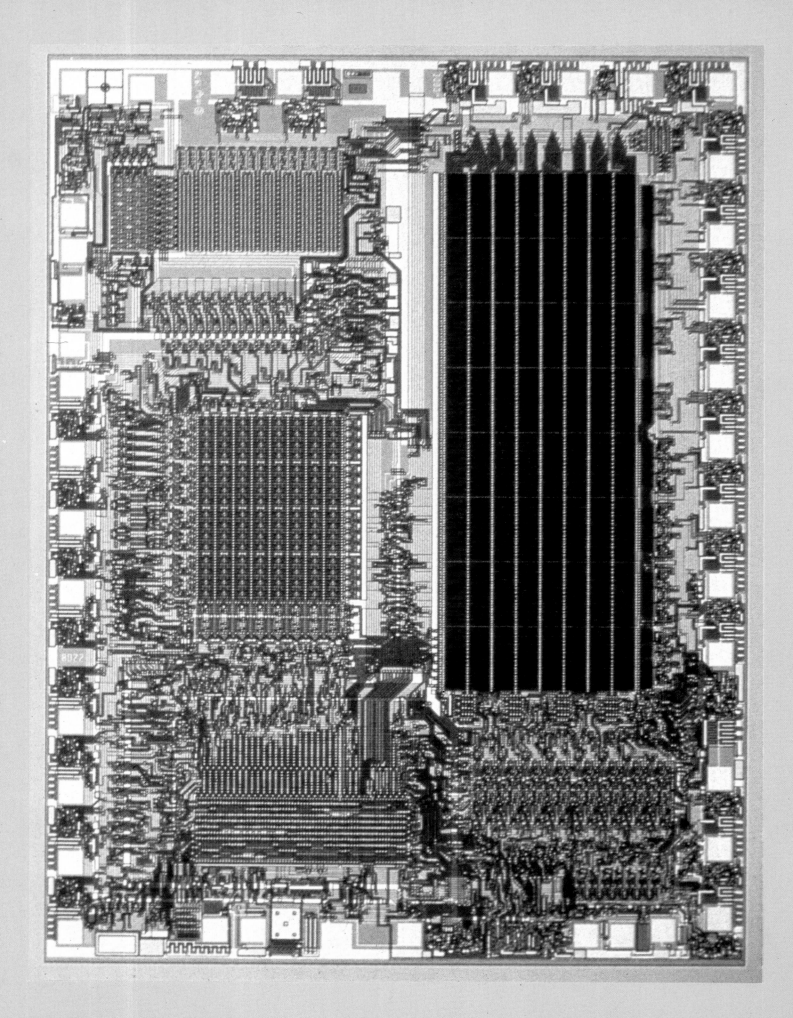

Above: A disc-shaped wafer before cutting, showing some of several hundred chips. It is compared in size with a watch movement. A chip can be programmed to act as a time-measurer itself, in the digital watch. The watch can not only keep time, but can also act as a stop watch, time-zone converter, lap recorder, alarm, calendar and calculator.

Some chips carry out only one aspect of computing, such as arithmetic operations. Others have the highly complex circuitry of a complete computer and can process and control information; these are 'computers on a chip' or microprocessors. The microprocessor shown opposite, enlarged 50 times, has different areas devoted to memory (the two large rectangles), and central processing (the rectangle at bottom right) which can perform more than 300 000 logical functions per second. The most advanced chips are capable of performing millions of logical operations per second.

than electron valves. Computer circuits containing transistors replaced those with electron valves, and computers shrank in size.

The scientists discovered that they could reduce whole electronic circuits and transfer them onto tiny pieces of silicon. As the circuits were much smaller, they could operate faster. Since then electronic circuits have been reduced in size to such an extent that tens of thousands of electronic components can be incorporated on a silicon wafer, or chip, only 5mm (¼ in) square.

The Miracle of Microprocessors
Some silicon chips can be used for the seperate functions of a computer such as the memory. Others incorporate circuits for both control and arithmetic processing as well as for memory. Called microprocessors, these are self-contained computers requiring only connections to input/output devices. Microprocessors form the basis of the pocket calculator, digital watch and desk-top computer.

By 1980 memory chips were being manufactured with a capacity of some 64 000 bits, while microprocessor chips had a capacity of up to 16 000 bits. They contained about 100 000 transistors, resistors and capacitors etched into their intricate circuitry. The way such chips are made is fascinating and is outlined on pages 56 and 57. It is not surprising that chip technology is considered 'magic'; a tiny 16 000 bit microprocessor has the computing power of

a room-size 1960s computer. And, whereas the 1960s computer could cost tens of thousands of pounds, the microprocessor costs less than £3 sterling.

It is the compactness and cheapness of the chip which is likely to bring about what might be the greatest industrial and social revolution in human history. It could be that future historians will catalogue human history in terms of life before and life after the chip: it is that important. There is also no danger that the raw material for chip-making will run out for, after oxygen, silicon is the most abundant element in the Earth's crust.

Chips for All
Microprocessors can provide us with extra brain power as and when we need it. They can relieve us of tedious labour. They are so small, so cheap and require so little energy to power them that there is virtually no limit to how many we can use or where we use them. They will almost certainly be present in almost every aspect of our lives. If the chip revolution spreads, every machine from the family car upwards will incorporate chips in its control mechanism. Engines will run more smoothly and require less fuel as chips regulate combustion and ignition. Automation will be applied to an ever-increasing extent as chip-controlled robots take over the bulk of industry's menial tasks. Everywhere throughout industry, the quality of products is likely to improve since measurement, accounting, adjusting and testing will be under chip control. There will be less wastage because the chip-controlled machines will operate to finer limits than before.

The Office of the Future
The office of the future will be almost cleared of paper because letters and inter-departmental memos will no longer pass to and fro. Instead, information will flow electronically between desk-top terminals within one company as well as from terminals in other companies. All the data that has to be filed at present will be stored on tape, ready for immediate transmission or recall at the press of a button. A master terminal in each office will combine functions of telephone, post, telex, document transmitter/receiver and photocopier. It may also be able to provide a facility for language translation.

Electronic letters will be typed on word processors and electronically dispatched to their destinations, simultaneously being filed at source. Word processors are already coming into use in present-day offices. As the typist types, the lines of type appear on a video screen. They can be corrected and re-written in any way. Then, at the touch of

a button, the machine types out the letter automatically, evenly, and with no errors. Word processors are also coming into use in newspaper offices, where they can be coupled with typesetting machines for automatic setting of 'copy'.

Working at Home

If electronic handling of information becomes the norm, there will be less need for the present type of office, staffed throughout the working day by people drawn from a wide area. The office of the future will only require a skeleton staff; most people will be able to work from home. This means that they will have their own home computer and communication terminal which can link up with a master console in the central office. They will then be able to use all the office audiovisual facilities remotely. Personal contacts will be made by videophone. The home office worker will have access to all kinds of information and reference material kept in extensive data banks which can be accessible through the computer.

The hardware for channelling all sorts of information into the home is already with us, through the teletext networks. These include Ceefax (BBC) and Prestel (Post Office) in Britain, Telidon in Canada, Infotext in the United States, and Antiope in France. These systems transmit information in the form of coded signals hidden in some of the lines that make up the ordinary television picture. Using a coupled electronic decoder, the information can be extracted and shown on the screen.

More Leisure Time

Whether working in the home-office or chip-controlled factories, workers will be highly productive and this will mean that they will be able to work much shorter hours to earn their living. Even within the present decade, a four-day working week will be introduced in some occupations, and in the 1990s this may well become the norm in a wide range of jobs. By then, the working year for many people could shrink to 40 weeks or less.

For centuries, workers have been used to working most of their days to maintain families and improve living standards. How will they cope with the abundant leisure time that tomorrow's world promises? Almost certainly some will take more than one job. One will be necessary to earn a living; the other is likely to have a vocational or interest value that is otherwise lacking in much working life. There will be more time to spend on favourite hobbies and sports, all of which are likely to become more and more popular. Tourism, too, will probably become another major growth area, as will self-education.

The hobbies, sports, education and 'knowledge' industries are thus likely to require many more people to organize and run them in the years ahead. This will help to compensate for the reduced labour force in some industries brought about by widespread automation. It follows the general drift in employment from manufacturing to service industries that is a feature of advanced technological civilizations.

Right: Workers will still be required in factories in the future, but in much smaller numbers and for shorter periods, thanks to automation. Working times will be more staggered so as to avoid the crush of rush hours.

Left: With more leisure and more wealth at their disposal, people may attempt more adventurous sports favoured at present by a minority.

Environment

Human beings consider themselves to be the most intelligent and best adapted creatures on our planet. Yet, surely, they are the most wasteful! On average, in Europe, each person produces nearly 1 kg (2.5 lbs) of waste material of one kind or another every day, from sewage and food waste to tin cans and plastic bags. The average American produces two to three times as much.

The Consumer Society

The waste occurs because we live in a predominantly consumer society. We consume vast quantities of goods; we use all manner of appliances and devices that improve our living standard; we drive cars to increase our mobility; and we seem to package virtually everything in paper, card or plastic film, or in disposable cans or bottles. The great majority of the items we buy are designed only to have a limited life and then to be thrown away. This is known as 'planned obsolescence'. It encourages good business profits but produces enormous waste. The disposal of this waste has grown into a massive worldwide problem, one that threatens the environment and, unchecked, could even lead to the eventual extinction of advanced life on our planet.

Careless release of wastes into the environment causes pollution, or gradual poisoning of that environment. Pollution of the land, the air, the rivers and the seas, is already well advanced. But in recent years there has been a greater awareness of the pollution problem which has led to stricter waste-disposal measures being adopted in many countries. People throughout the world are beginning to combat pollution through a United Nations environmental protection agency.

Land Pollution

Pollution of the land can take several forms. There is, for example, poisoning of the land caused by careless disposal of industrial wastes, including deadly chemicals like cyanide, cadmium and mercury compounds and dangerous organic materials. Eventually, these might be carried by the action of ground water into reservoirs and find their way, with disastrous consequences into drinking water.

Having identified the sources of industrial pollution, we can take steps to combat it, and this is already being done. Industrial pollution is being curbed at its source in factories throughout the world. Moreover, it is now realized that remedial measures can be made to pay for themselves. Processing wastes can recover valuable chemicals that can then be recycled.

Left: Unrestricted strip mining can devastate the countryside, resulting in a barren landscape that offends the eye. In some locations, however, it is possible to remould the wasted landscape to advantage. Sometimes this is made a condition before mining is allowed to proceed.

Below: A scene with which we are all too familiar – carelessly discarded rubbish at the water's edge. Legislation alone cannot control such thoughtless behaviour; everyone must become more conscious of the environment.

Above: Built to last for only a few years, the modern car is a typical product of our consumer society. Millions are consigned to the scrap heap every year to make way for newer, but not appreciably better, models. Such a 'throw-away' philosophy is very wasteful of raw materials unless they are recycled.

Deadly Pesticides

Another form of pollution can result as a side effect of chemical fertilization. Potash and nitrate fertilizers which are applied in large quantities to agricultural land improve crop production, but any surplus drains from the land into rivers where they cause a rapid increase in weed growth. The weeds use up the available oxygen in the water with the result that fish and other wildlife can no longer survive. This effect is called eutrophication. The use of chemical pesticides on agricultural land can have another deadly effect. They often become concentrated in a natural food chain – e.g. from seed dressing, to sparrow, to sparrowhawk – leading to the death or sterilization of the last link in the chain.

New Methods of Control

Crop scientists are continuing to improve their knowledge of fertilizers and chemical sprays. They can now judge more accurately how to apply them, and they choose chemicals that have little effect on harmless living things. In recent years, many insecticides have been banned in most places, including DDT and Dieldrin,

because of their effects on other living creatures, and more harmless ones have been substituted. In some instances biological methods have replaced chemical methods of control with spectacular results. Once again, genetic engineering (see page 27) may come to the rescue in the long term and solve both the pest and fertilizer problems.

There are also other aspects to land pollution. There is the destruction of the countryside by mining and quarrying activities, which may result in desolate landscapes and ugly spoil heaps. Wastelands may result from bad agricultural practice, and deforestation and over-grazing may make the land barren and easily eroded (see page 18).

Reclamations

It is possible for a mined landscape to be sympathetically restored if not to its former state, then to something equally good or even better. This already happens where strip mining takes place close to settled communities. The layer of soil which is stripped from above the deposit before the mining begins is afterwards replaced and re-planted. Worked-out gravel pits can have their edges planted with trees and plants and can be filled with water to form lakes that are a haven for wildlife and a delight for the local population. Sensible farming practice can often return agricultural wastelands to productive use. They can be provided with shelter belts of trees, planted with soil-binding plants and cultivated in ways that combat erosion, e.g. by contour farming and terracing.

All at Sea

Rivers pick up waste as they flow past industrial and urban areas. Factories often discharge untreated chemical wastes directly into rivers, and towns may pipe in raw sewage which pollutes and de-oxygenates the water. Discharge of raw sewage directly into the sea is also commonplace, the assumption being that the seas are so vast that they can absorb and disperse any amount of waste materials. This is not true.

The Mediterranean Sea is already so polluted that bathing is banned in some places. The vast sea-like Great Lakes in North America are nearly devoid of life because industries around them have poured in pollutants for years. In the past, rivers flowing into them have been so full of inflammable chemicals that they have even been known to catch fire. It has been said of some waters that people falling into them were more likely to die from poisoning than drowning. But in recent years the pollution tide has turned. Much stricter control is now being exercised in many areas over the disposal of industrial waste, and many local authorities now require factories and sewage disposal plants to treat effluents before discharging them into rivers or the sea so that they will not cause pollution.

Oil Pollution

The demand for crude oil also poses problems for the environment. More and more oil tankers are plying the oceans, and they are becoming so big that they are difficult to manoeuvre. Supertanker accidents and collisions are on the increase. In 1978, the *Amoco Cadiz* ran aground off Brittany, spilling some 220 000 tonnes of crude oil into the sea. Hundreds of kilometres of French coastline were polluted with appalling effects on seabirds and other marine and coastal life. Incidents of this kind have led to increased safety standards but the dangers persist.

More intensive offshore production also increases the risk of oil-pollution, as was demonstrated by the 'blow-outs' in the great Ekofisk field in the North Sea and in the Gulf of Campeche, off Mexico, in the late 1970s.

Right: The destruction of the *Torrey Canyon* in 1967 was the first of the big oil tanker disasters, which have since polluted the seas with millions of tonnes of crude oil. Stricter regulations governing the transportation of oil as well as effective dispersal techniques to deal with spills could help combat pollution of this kind.

Left: Natural gas is burned off at an oil field. It is not only wasteful of a dwindling natural resource, but also harms the environment by discharging carbon dioxide and unburned hydro-carbons into the atmosphere.

If the world 'goes nuclear' in a big way to offset the energy crisis, a new pollution threat will come to the fore – radioactivity. The wastes from nuclear plants are intensely radioactive and remain so for hundreds of years. Disposal of these wastes is already beginning to be a problem. Until now they have been sealed in drums and dumped at sea or buried underground. But these methods cannot be practised on a large scale and are suspect because containers are subject to leakage. A more promising method is to convert the wastes into glass that will remain stable indefinitely.

Such massive oil spills are very difficult to deal with. Anti-pollution teams have had some success in preventing them from spreading by using floating dispersants. Early dispersants caused as much damage to the environment as the oil, but the newer types coming into use are more effective and less toxic. There is also some evidence that natural processes eventually break down the oil into less harmful products and the action of bacteria may also be effective in some cases, but this takes a long time. It is possible that treatment with specially designed bacteria may offer the best long-term solution to oil pollution. We cannot ignore the possibility, however, that the world will run out of oil before the pollution problem becomes manageable.

Air Pollution

Our most popular machine, the car, is responsible for many undesirable changes in our environment. Cars require extensive networks of road than can mar the landscape. Traffic clogs the city streets and also produces a great deal of noise that can make living in a city unpleasant. But the greatest problem is that cars cause serious air pollution.

When petrol burns with air in a car engine poisonous gases such as carbon monoxide and nitrogen oxides are produced. In addition, most petrol contains lead tetraethyl, an organic compound added to improve combustion. When petrol burns, harmful lead compounds are released into the air. The unburned petrol and smoke particles in the vehicle exhaust are acted upon by sunlight to form a murky cloud which can build up into a thick smog. This is most serious in natural hollows, like the Los Angeles basin, where stagnant air pockets form and trap the pollutants. Exhaust fumes, with or without smog, can have a serious effect on health. They are indirectly responsible for thousands of deaths every year through bronchitis and other respiratory illnesses, and countless millions of workdays lost.

Anti-Pollution Devices

The car engine is now being cleaned up in various ways to reduce harmful exhaust emissions. Crankcase breathers, manifold reactors and catalytic convertors are among the anti-pollution devices now being tried. Some car engines have been slightly modified so that they can function equally well on lead-free petrol. The great drawback about these measures is that they tend to increase petrol consumption, which is most undesirable in our energy-conscious age. Answers seem to lie in (1) redesigning the car engine to burn petrol more efficiently, (2) eventually replacing petrol as fuel and (3) replacing the internal combustion engine with a non-polluting power source (see page 35).

Industry also burns vast amounts of the fossil fuels – coal, oil and natural gas – which results in a great deal of air

65

pollution. One major additional cause of pollution from this source is the acid gas, sulphur dioxide. This corrodes metal in damp air and eats away building stone, as many cities know to their cost. Increasingly now, however, this kind of pollution is being curbed at the source by devices which absorb gases in furnace flues and extract harmful particles.

The Greenhouse Effect

One major pollutant, carbon dioxide, remains. This gas exists naturally in the air and, in small quantities, is harmless. But the amount of carbon dioxide in the air is progressively increasing, and there is a danger that the build-up of the gas will affect the climate. There are signs that it is causing what is known as the greenhouse effect. Carbon dioxide traps more of the heat of the Sun in the lower atmosphere and appreciably warms the climate. This could eventually trigger off all manner of changes in weather patterns and even melt the polar ice caps, which would cause disastrous flooding. No-one knows the real extent of the problem, or its consequences. It might even be that, if controlled, the greenhouse effect could be beneficial. Some climatologists believe that, were it not for the slight warming that has occurred in the atmosphere in recent times, the Earth might slip into another Ice Age.

The Ozone Layer

Another potential hazard of air pollution is that the ozone layer in the atmosphere will be thinned or destroyed. This layer, which exists some 30 km (20 miles) above the Earth's surface filters out the bulk of the harmful ultra-violet radiation from the Sun. If the amount of this radiation were greatly increased due to a thinning of the ozone layer, it is likely that there would be an enormous increase in skin cancer among human beings. Weather patterns around the world would also be greatly affected.

There are several things that threaten the ozone layer. One is high-flying supersonic planes. The engines release directly into the high-atmosphere, or stratosphere, copious amounts of nitrogen oxide. This gas attacks ozone and converts it to ordinary oxygen. Another threat is space rockets. Solid booster rockets, of the type used in the space-shuttle, emit large amounts of chlorine, which can also destroy ozone. Chlorine is also sprayed into the atmosphere in aerosol sprays, for the propellant is a compound like Freon (dichlorodi-fluoromethane), better known as a coolant in refrigerators.

Fortunately, the aerosol threat is not as great as it once was, for there is now strict control on the use of aerosol propellants

The ravages of air pollution are clearly evident on this stone sculpture. Sulphur dioxide is one of the worst industrial pollutants and forms acid in moist air. This acid readily eats away building stones like limestones and marble.

Right: Ancient buildings like the pyramid tombs and statues of ancient Egypt must be treasured and preserved for future generations. When they are threatened with destruction, we must try to save them. This happened with the temples at Abu Simbel built by Rameses II in the 13th century BC. They were removed from their original site, which was going to be flooded by the rising waters of the reservoir behind the Aswan dam.

throughout the world. There are unlikely to be large fleets of supersonic airliners flying the skies, as was once thought, and relatively few shuttles will be commuting into space as they are very expensive. Also, there is some evidence to suggest that the ozone level naturally remains broadly in balance, with any ozone loss being balanced by ozone production. The problem remains, however, that we do not really know enough about the chemical reactions that take place in the ozone layer, so we must continue to be cautious.

Preserving Wildlife

The possible harmful effects of insecticides on wildlife has already been mentioned (page 63). But human beings endanger a wide variety of species both directly and indirectly. Over the centuries, people have destroyed animal life in many ways. They have hunted many species to extinction, the most notorious example being the dodo. Recently they have threatened the tiger and other big 'cats', the elephant, the whale, polar bear, oryx and orang-utan, as well as a host of other creatures.

The threat has not only come from chemicals and hunting but from the destruction of habitats by civil engineering works – building roads, dams and new towns, for example – or by thoughtless forestry and agriculture. The destruction of habitat perhaps poses the most serious threat to wildlife in general. The tropical rain forest, home for a multitude of exotic creatures, is particularly threatened. It has been calculated that it is being destroyed at the rate of some 20 hectares (50 acres) per minute.

To the Rescue!

Fortunately, concern for hundreds of threatened species is now worldwide, and most countries are taking steps to ensure

their survival. International organizations like the World Wildlife Fund (WWF) are helping to influence world opinion and co-ordinate rescue operations and conservation movements. Since 1961, the WWF has rescued 33 mammals and birds from the brink of extinction. It has contributed more than £20 000 000 ($40 000 000) to conservation projects around the world, and it has created or supported over 250 national parks on five continents, covering a total area of nearly twice the size of Western Europe.

But in spite of splendid efforts, there are still creatures and plants in danger. It is estimated that nearly 300 mammals, almost 300 birds, 100 reptiles, 125 plants, 80 fishes and 30 amphibians are endangered even today. If the Earth is to remain rich in wildlife in the future, vigilance must continue to be practised to ensure the safety of the creatures and plants that live there.

Top left: Many plant species are vulnerable when areas are developed. Botanists are striving to build up a seed bank of endangered specimens from which seedlings can be raised and eventually transplanted back into decimated areas.

Above: The giant panda has become the trademark of the World Wildlife Fund, one of the most important organizations intent on preserving endangered species of wildlife. The giant panda, of which only a few remain, is a native of China, where it is now afforded complete protection. Like many of the other threatened species, its main enemy is human beings.

Life in Space

Left: The shuttle orbiter blasts off the launch pad on top of the external fuel tank which provides the fuel for its three main engines. The strap-on booster rockets on the side of the tank fire too, producing a combined take-off thrust of some 3 million kg (7 million lb).

We have been able to travel into space for only a short time, yet many people believe that ultimately our future lies there. Only by venturing farther into space and by mastering the space environment will the population be able to continue to grow in the centuries to come.

At the beginning of the Space Age, it was feared that people would not be able to survive in space for long. Our bodies have been designed for life on Earth, where gravity keeps our feet firmly on the ground and the atmosphere provides us with life-giving oxygen and protection from radiation. In space there is a near vacuum. There is nothing to shield us from extreme heat (in sunlight), extreme cold (in the shade), harmful radiation and meteoritic particles. We must take our 'atmosphere' with us to survive. When we are in orbit, we feel no gravity at all – we are weightless. In contrast, when we are rocketed into orbit, the powerful acceleration subjects our bodies to a force three or more times stronger than Earth's gravity. We

Right: The orbiter has shed its booster rockets and external fuel tank and is floating in orbit. It is seen launching a large satellite by means of its remote-controlled manipulating arm. Its voluminous cargo bay can carry loads 18 metres (60ft) long and 4.6 metres (15ft) across.

Left: Its mission completed, the shuttle re-enters the atmosphere and glides to a runway landing. Within a fortnight it will be ready to return to orbit.

Opposite: In the 21st century the shuttle will ferry people and materials to the mammoth structures that will be assembled in space to serve the expanding Earth population.

experience a similar high 'g-force' on returning to Earth, when the craft has to slow down rapidly.

Space Endurance
Can the human body withstand such stresses for long periods? The answer is that it can. Since the 1960s, American and Russian astronauts and cosmonauts have undertaken longer and longer missions in space in such craft as the American Skylab and the Russian Salyut. At the beginning of the 1980s, the space endurance record stood at 175 days, achieved by the cosmonauts Vladimir Lyakhov and Valery Ryukin in the Salyut 6 orbital station, ferried by the Soyuz 34 spacecraft. While they were there fresh fuel and supplies were delivered by automatic space transports, named Progress.

Like the Skylab astronauts before them, the Salyut cosmonauts carried out scores of

experiments in the physical sciences, engineering, biology and medicine, and also carried out astronomical observations and Earth-survey work. The results they obtained suggest that there would be much to gain from permanent Earth-orbiting stations.

Observatories in Orbit
It has already been mentioned that huge space structures such as communications platforms and solar power satellites will play a major role in the world of tomorrow. So will orbiting astronomical observation platforms, which will enable us to peer far deeper into space than at present. We shall be able to observe the universe clearly for there is no atmosphere to absorb the radiation or distort the view. Orbiting industrial modules will also have their place. They will be able to exploit the zero-gravity environment, abundant solar power and the vacuum and cold of space in order to

produce such things as super-pure and super-strong metals.

A True Space Vehicle

Building a space station of any appreciable size would naturally involve the transfer of a great many workers and large amounts of materials between the Earth and the site of construction orbit. Early ferry craft, such as Soyuz and Apollo (the American craft developed for the Moon-landing missions in the 1960s and 1970s) would not be good enough. Not only are they too small, but they are representative of a 'throw-away' technology that the world of tomorrow cannot afford. The answer is already with us in the form of the space shuttle, perhaps the first true space vehicle.

Reusable Shuttle

The first-generation shuttle has already begun work and will carry on into the 1990s. Unlike previous space transports, the shuttle is reusable. It is at one and the same time rocket, spacecraft and aeroplane. The main part of the shuttle is a delta-winged orbiter, of similar dimensions to a medium-range airliner like the DC-9. It rides into space on top of a huge fuel tank, to which booster rockets are attached.

The orbiter's main engines and booster rockets fire together at lift-off, and then the boosters separate and parachute to Earth to be used again. The fuel tank, however, is jettisoned just before the orbiter goes into orbit and is the only part of the shuttle system not to be reused. At the end of the space mission the orbiter fires retro-rockets to slow it down and allow it to return to Earth. The atmosphere slows the orbiter down until it is able to use its wings to glide to a runway landing.

Even the present orbiter has a large carrying capacity. Its huge cargo bay can house structures up to 18 metres (60 ft) long and 4.5 metres (15 ft) in diameter, weighing as much as 30 tonnes, and later versions will be even bigger. Some may well be fitted out as passenger transports if the large space stations come into use. One transport capable of carrying 74 space travellers has already been designed.

The shuttle's present duties involve launching satellites and servicing or retrieving those that have stopped working. One of its main cargoes is the space laboratory Spacelab, designed by the European Space Agency for month-long experimental missions. Soon this or later generation shuttles will begin ferrying purpose-built cylindrical modules into orbit to be assembled there into prototype space stations. Almost certainly this is how the first permanent orbiting stations will be built, for no new technology is needed.

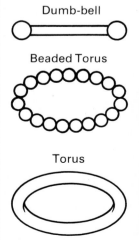

Dumb-bell

Beaded Torus

Torus

Left: Some of the possible designs for future space habitats. Of these the simple torus, or wheel shape finds most favour. The finished structure might look like that in the picture below. The central 'hub' houses solar power and docking facilities and mirrors to reflect sunlight into the living areas.

Modular Space Stations

Space stations could be constructed by docking or linking the modules together either end-to-end or to a central unit. They could all be equipped with other docking hatches so that ferry craft could use them or other modules could be attached to expand the station. Later, if more ambitious space projects get under way, heavy launching vehicles may be developed to ferry loads of hundreds of tonnes into orbit. Like the shuttle, they would be reusable.

While the early orbiting stations might be assembled from modules prefabricated on Earth, this would not be possible with

later space structures, which would be huge constructions measuring several kilometres across. These massive structures would be fabricated on site in orbit from materials ferried in bulk from Earth. Designs for a robot 'beam builder' are already well advanced. This would produce the metal girders that form the skeletal framework of most space structures.

Aluminium will probably be the material used for construction because its lightness makes it easier to lift into space, but there is much to be said in favour of steel. Though it is heavier and therefore more costly to lift into orbit, once there it is

Above: The view inside the outer tube of a huge torus habitat. As with all designs, the torus is rotated around the hub to create artificial gravity. The centrifugal force set up by rotation keeps the land and water pressed 'down' away from the hub. 'Up' is towards the hub.

just as easy to handle and is much easier to work with than aluminium. In space there is no atmosphere to corrode and weaken steel structures as there is on Earth. In addition, whereas readily available aluminium ore is already scarce on Earth, there is plenty of iron ore.

Cities in Space

Orbiting space stations would be located several hundred kilometres above the Earth, in a relatively close orbit, serving as a springboard for the next stage of expansion into space – the creation of permanent space habitats, or colonies. These would not be sited close to the Earth, but in a region in space at a distance of 350 000 kilometres (240 000 miles) from both the Earth and the Moon.

This region lies at one corner of an imaginary equilateral triangle, with the Earth and Moon at the other corners. It is known as a Lagrangian point, and is one of five such regions within the Earth-Moon system. At a Lagrangian point, Earth and lunar gravity interact in such a way as to 'lock' in position any body placed there. This gravitational lock would ensure that the space colony would never wander.

Idle Dreams

Space colonies are not simply idle dreams any more, but projects being seriously considered for early in the 21st century. Several suitable designs have been worked out, and the astonishing thing is that we could even start building them now, given enough money.

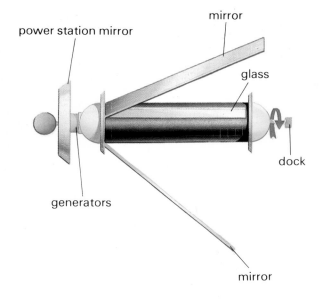

power station mirror

mirror

glass

generators

dock

mirror

A cylindrical habitat which rotates around its long axis is favoured by Gerard O'Neill. Two identical habitats are linked together to form a single colony. This helps to lessen the colonists' feeling of isolation. The land areas in the habitat occupy three broad strips running lengthwise down the cylinder. Opposite them are three transparent windows to let in the sunlight. The sunlight is reflected into the windows by three huge mirrors, hinged to one end of the cylinder. The angle of the mirrors can be adjusted to give cycles of day and night and seasonal variations in temperature.

Intensive agriculture is practised in the body of the cylinder and also in the smaller cylindrical agricultural pods set in a circular ring outside. The complex shown at the end of the cylinder to the right of the picture houses docking, communications and control facilities. At the other end of the cylinder are solar furnaces for power production, together with essential industrial units. Industrial activities also take place in the external pods.

Of the numerous colony designs proposed, the wheel and cylinder types seem to offer the most benefits. One wheel- or torus-shaped habitat proposed by NASA consists of a tube of 130 metres (430 ft) cross-section, formed into a ring some 1800 metres (over 1 mile) in diameter. This houses the main living and agricultural areas and is capable of supporting as many as 10 000 people. 'Spokes' connect the tube to a central hub. Attached to the hub above and below are docking ports, aerial arrays and industrial modules, together with radiators to rid the habitat of excess heat.

Controlled Environment

The 'wheel' is rotated once a minute, to simulate gravity. The landscape is held by the artificial gravity on the inner surface of the tube away from the hub – 'up' is towards the hub and 'down' away from it. Above the hub is a large stationary mirror inclined at an angle of 45°. It reflects the perpetual sunlight in space into louvred windows running all the way along the tube. With the help of this ceaseless sunshine, the colonists can practise intensive agriculture, cropping several times a year in a carefully controlled environment. The sunlight also provides the energy to drive the turbogenerators which produce the colony's electricity.

The cylindrical habitat design shown here is favoured by Gerard O'Neill, an American physicist. A pair of cylinders forms a colony. The land areas are arranged in three strips on the side of the cylinders, which again rotate to simulate gravity. Sunlight is reflected through the huge windows by hinged mirrors that separate the land areas.

Minerals from the Moon

Both space colony proposals rely on the Moon as a source of materials. It would be much easier and cheaper to ferry materials from the Moon than from the Earth, since lunar gravity is only one-sixth that of the Earth, and on the Earth many minerals are already becoming scarce. The materials mined on the Moon could be transported to the colony construction site in an ingenious way, by a kind of electromagnetic catapult called the mass driver. The material would be scooped up in buckets which would accelerate along a track by magnetic waves to beyond lunar escape velocity (about 2.5 kilometres, 1.5 miles, a second). Then the buckets would be slowed down, causing the material inside to be ejected into space, 'caught' and carried by space tug to the construction site.

Metals such as iron and aluminium could then be extracted from the lunar soil and processed in factories for use on construction sites in space.

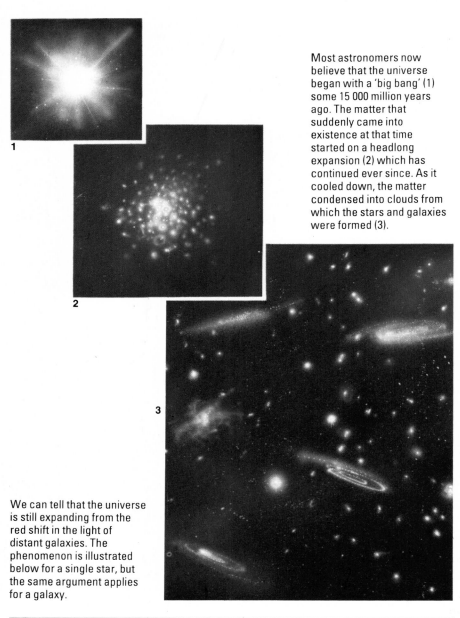

Most astronomers now believe that the universe began with a 'big bang' (1) some 15 000 million years ago. The matter that suddenly came into existence at that time started on a headlong expansion (2) which has continued ever since. As it cooled down, the matter condensed into clouds from which the stars and galaxies were formed (3).

We can tell that the universe is still expanding from the red shift in the light of distant galaxies. The phenomenon is illustrated below for a single star, but the same argument applies for a galaxy.

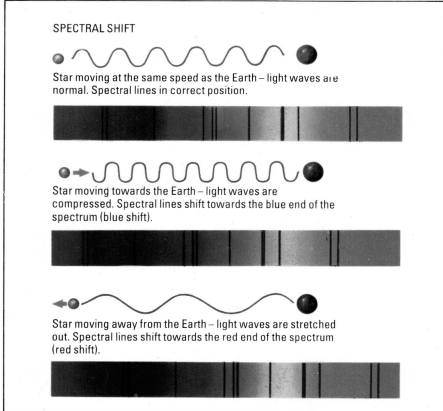

SPECTRAL SHIFT

Star moving at the same speed as the Earth – light waves are normal. Spectral lines in correct position.

Star moving towards the Earth – light waves are compressed. Spectral lines shift towards the blue end of the spectrum (blue shift).

Star moving away from the Earth – light waves are stretched out. Spectral lines shift towards the red end of the spectrum (red shift).

Mysteries of the Universe

If there are cities floating in space and bases on the Moon, people in the 21st century might think that they are well on the way to solving all the puzzles of the universe. But that is a vain thought. The universe is so vast and so complex that it will always hold mysteries to baffle us. It seems that the more we probe, the more mysteries are revealed.

It was once thought that the Earth was the centre of a spherical universe, with Sun, Moon, planets and stars circling around it. Later, when the Earth had been relegated to the role of a humble planet, the universe became little larger than the solar system. Then astronomers began calculating the distance to the stars and realized that we inhabited a galaxy of stars, and the universe became the galaxy. Eventually, multitudes of other galaxies were discovered in the black void of space. As telescopes increased in power, more galaxies came into view. So the known universe appeared bigger and bigger.

How Big is the Universe?

The universe is bigger than we can ever imagine! Distances in space are so colossal that we need a much bigger measuring unit than kilometres or miles. A convenient one is the distance travelled by light in a certain time. In our everyday lives think of light travelling instantaneously, but it has a finite speed. We can express astronomical distances in terms of the distance light travels in a second, say, or an hour, or a year, calling these units light-seconds, light-hours, and so on. On this scale one light-second is about 30 000 km, one light-hour is 11 million km and one light-year nearly 10 million km (respectively 186 000, 700 million and 6 million million miles).

Using this scale, we can get an idea of the scale of the universe. Our neighbour the Moon lies 1½ light-seconds away from us. The Sun lies a little over 8 light-minutes away. The farthest planet Pluto lies 5½ light-hours away. Staggeringly, the nearest star lies no less than 4½ light-years away!

The Edge of the Universe

Our galaxy, which is made up of something like 100 000 million stars, measures about 100 000 light-years across. One of the few other galaxies we can see with the naked eye, the Andromeda, lies 2 million light-years away, and the farthest galaxies lie thousands of millions of light-years away. The most distant astronomical objects of all are not ordinary galaxies but much smaller, yet much brighter bodies called quasars. The most distant quasars appear to be over 15 000 million light-years away.

Is this the edge of the universe? Is there an edge at all? What shape is the universe? How did it begin? These are all questions that remain unanswered. Einstein's revolutionary theories of relativity suggest that the universe is curved and is changing. It may be curved outward in the form of a hyperboloid, or saddle. In which case, it would extend indefinitely in all directions. Or it may be curved inwards in the form of a sphere. In which case it would be finite in extent.

Is the Universe Changing?

In our own brief lifetimes the heavens do not appear to change very much. Yet astronomers find convincing evidence that the universe as a whole is getting bigger all the time, as Einstein's theories suggest it might. This evidence is the 'red shift' in the light we receive from distant galaxies.

When light passes through a spectroscope, it divides into a rainbow band of colours that tell astronomers a great deal about the star or planet emitting the light. Earlier this century astronomers found that light from distant galaxies was more red than they had expected. Dark lines in the spectrum of the light are shifted towards the red end of the spectrum. This red shift is caused, astronomers think, by the galaxies moving away from us. We have all experienced a similar shift, in sound, when a blaring police car siren first approaches, then goes away from us. The pitch of the sound changes, making the sound of the receding siren lower, as though the sound waves are being 'stretched out'. The stretching out of light waves from a receding galaxy reddens the light.

The Beginning

Not only do we find that the galaxies are speeding away from us but we also find that the more distant they are, the faster they are travelling, and the greater is their red shift. By observing the red shift for nearby galaxies whose distance we know, we can calculate the relationship between red shift and distance, and by measuring the red shift of other galaxies, we can deduce their distance from us.

The red shift observations provide evidence that the universe is expanding. We must therefore assume that it was once smaller than it is now. By going backwards in time, we can pinpoint when such an expansion began from a central point. It works out at between about 15 000 and

20 000 million years ago. Some cosmologists consider that this is when the universe began.

The Big Bang

It is convenient to think of the beginning of the universe as a gigantic explosion in which all space and matter was hurled outwards. We call this concept the big-bang theory. Before the big bang, it is thought, nothing existed – no matter, no space, no time.

The theory suggests that at the moment of the big bang all the matter in the universe was very hot. As the universe expanded, it cooled. It has been calculated that by now the average temperature of space should be about 3 degrees above absolute zero ($-270°C$). In 1965 radio astronomers discovered a general background radiation in space which corresponded to this temperature. It provided the most convincing evidence yet of a big-bang beginning to the universe.

The main alternative theory about the origin of the universe, the steady-state theory, cannot adequately explain the observed background radiation and has now largely been abandoned. The theory accepts that the universe is expanding, but suggests that it has always done so and

Star formation is still going on today in the giant clouds, or nebulae, that exist between the stars. We can see one of these clouds with the naked eye in the star constellation we call Orion, the Mighty Hunter. The Orion nebula lies about 1500 light-years away from us and is about 16 light-years across. It is located in the constellation below Orion's 'belt'.

always will. But over all, the universe remains the same since matter is continually being created to maintain a steady state. For a steady-state universe, there was no beginning and will be no end.

What is Matter?

Broadly speaking, we see our present universe as concentrations – clouds or lumps – of matter moving in space. Matter is anything that takes up space – a solid, a liquid or a gas. It is made up of very tiny, invisible particles called atoms. There are more than a hundred known chemical elements each made up of a different kind of atom.

Atoms join with other atoms to form the molecules that make up matter or substance. A molecule is the smallest part of a substance that can exist. All of the different substances we find on Earth are made up of molecules formed from combinations of different atoms.

How did these different atoms come into being? It is thought that during the big bang matter was created in the form of the simplest atomic particles – protons, electrons and neutrons – that form the heart, or nucleus, of all atoms. In the searing heat of the big bang, many of the protons and neutrons fused together in a nuclear reaction to create the element – helium. From the expanding mass of hydrogen and helium the present universe evolved. These elements are still the most plentiful in the universe.

What's Inside the Atom?

Only a century ago such a question would have been regarded as stupid because the atom was considered the smallest bit of matter there was. The word atom means 'that which cannot be cut'. But nothing could be further from the truth. Early this century it was discovered that the atom is made up of a basic nucleus containing two particles – neutrons, with no electric charge; and protons, with a positive electric charge. Around the nucleus spins a cloud of tinier particles with a negative electric charge – electrons.

Throughout this century physicists and mathematicians have increased our knowledge of atoms even further. The picture of the atom became so complex that it could only be 'illustrated' with mathematics. By bombarding the atom with protons, for example, physicists found they could knock particles from the nucleus and actually change one atom into another. Gradually, more sophisticated and powerful devices called accelerators were built to increase the speed of bombardment, and scientists were staggered to find that all kinds of new particles were given off. At present over 200 elementary atomic particles have been identified and our picture of matter has been totally altered once again.

Baffling Particles

There appear to be two main types of particles in the atom – hadrons and leptons. There are scores of hadrons, including the proton, neutron, pion and kaon; some are electrically charged, others not. But there are only four leptons known: the electron, the muon, and two types of neutrino. The neutrino is one of the most baffling particles, having no mass or charge, only the energy of spin. But that is not the end of the complexity of the atom.

It now appears that the hadrons themselves are divisible and are different combinations of at least four more fundamental particles called quarks. Though they have not yet been positively identified in atomic collisions, they have been named the 'up', 'down', 'strange' and 'charmed' quarks.

Research is already proceeding on the development of even more sophisticated instruments that will enable scientists to discover even more about the atom. As each new particle comes to light physicists will be ever closer to their goal of revealing the indivisible elements of the universe.

The Riddle of Life

Just as nuclear physicists have unravelled some of the secrets of the atom, so biologists have begun to gain insight into the mystery of life. Not so long ago it was believed that life was a miracle that defied scientific explanation. Then, with the growth of organic chemistry, it became possible to explain life processes in terms of basic chemistry. The clue to the processes is the extraordinary nature of the carbon atom which is able to form literally millions of compounds by combing with other carbon atoms and, mainly, atoms of hydrogen and oxygen. The organic compounds it forms make up most of the food we eat, most of the living parts of plants and animals, and, most importantly, most of each human being. In living things, the organic compounds formed by carbon atoms are the main source of the warmth and energy we need to live.

DNA

The basic unit of all living things is the cell. Each human being consists of about 100 million million cells all of which originated from a single cell – the fertilized egg cell. How does that, or any other single cell, grow into a complex organism? The answer lies in the chemical structure of a special molecule in the nucleus of the cell. It is called DNA.

The DNA molecule is incredibly complex and takes the shape of a double helix or spiral. The sub-units of DNA, the genes, carry hereditary characteristics from one generation to another, ensuring that coded information is passed on from cell to cell as they divide to make more cells. Genes also order the manufacture of the proteins that occur inside every living cell.

Vital Proteins

While an organism's genes prescribe both the development and the chemical reactions by which its body works, the process of protein manufacture they control is vital. The word 'protein' is derived from a Greek word meaning 'first' and expresses the fundamental nature of

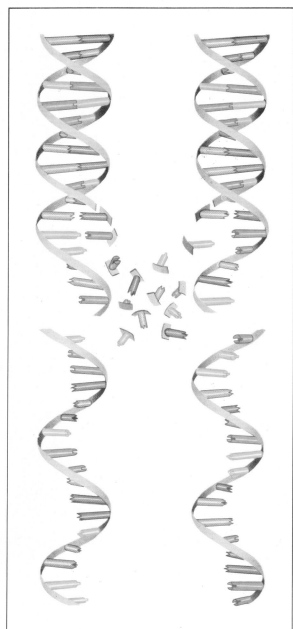

When DNA replicates, or makes copies of itself, each of its unwound strands (top) builds a second strand out of the four types of building blocks or chemical bases.

Normally, the two helical strands of DNA remain linked together, but they can unwind from one another as shown. This happens in the cell nucleus whenever a cell is about to divide and multiply.

the protein molecule. But why are they so important?

We know that one main function of some proteins is body-building. Other kinds of proteins have an equally vital but entirely different function. These proteins are the body's enzymes which enable the many millions of cells in the human body to keep each cell alive and healthy. Precisely how they do this is a mystery that still eludes the scientists who study them. Proteins are therefore among the most intriguing group of substances that exist.

Is there Life Elsewhere?

We now know a great deal about life processes and how they work, but how did life begin in the first place? Is it likely that there is life elsewhere in the universe? When the Earth began some 5000 million years ago, it is thought to have been a ball of molten rock and steam surrounded by an atmosphere of poisonous gases and water vapour. It seems impossible that any form of life could have existed on Earth then.

Later, when the Earth cooled down, it is thought that the action of sunlight and lightning on the gases – ammonia, methane and hydrogen – and on water vapour in

Above: Astronomers use massive radio telescopes like this 100-metre (328ft) dish at Effelsberg, West Germany, to pick up radio 'messages' from distant stars. From its infancy in the 1930s, radio astronomy has become one of the most exciting branches of astronomy, showing astronomers a different kind of universe, populated by enigmatic bodies such as quasars and pulsars, as well as ordinary stars.

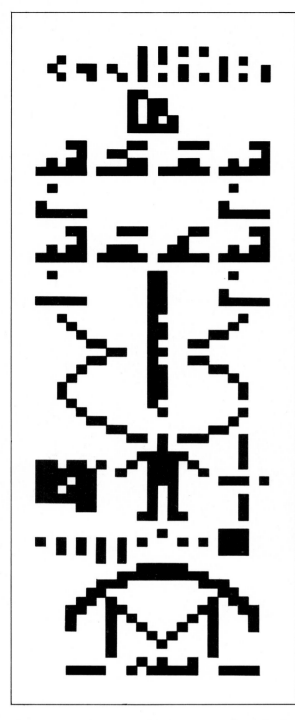

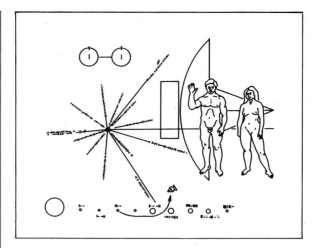

Left: In case any other intelligent beings anywhere in the universe should find them, the Pioneer space probes to Jupiter carried plaques like this to identify their senders. The star-like diagram in the centre left gives the position of the Sun in relation to prominent pulsars, while the diagram at the bottom depicts the solar system. The figures show human form and stature relative to the Pioneer probe.

the atmosphere could have produced the basic organic chemical from which the first living things evolved. Since 1953 scientists have been able to produce simple proteins, the basic building blocks of living things, in laboratory experiments imitating the conditions in the early atmosphere. Over hundreds of millions of years, ever more complex organic chemicals would have been formed on Earth, eventually including those which could reproduce themselves. These were possibly similar to mud-living bacteria today. These bacteria eventually gave rise to the first plant-like organisms.

If life on Earth did come about as the result of such a process, it seems more than likely that life could exist elsewhere in the universe. The more scientists learn about the universe through their powerful telescopes, satellites and probes, the more convinced they become that there is other life. With their radio telescopes, for example, they have already discovered a host of organic molecules and water vapour in the gas clouds that exist in our galaxy. Some meteorites contain organic chemicals and might even contain fossils of primitive micro-organisms. It is even believed by some people that 'life spores' of some sort exist in space and give rise to life processes when they find suitable planets to receive them.

Whether this is so or not, there are almost certainly many planets similar to the Earth in the universe. Astronomers have already discovered that some of the nearer stars have planetary systems. Could these contain planets similar to the Earth and beings similar to people? We do not know.

In the hope that some intelligent creature somewhere in the universe may be listening, some astronomers have beamed coded messages out into space. They are also listening for intelligible signals from space. One day – tomorrow, next year, next century – such signals could arrive, telling us we are not alone in the universe.

Above: One of the many 'genuine' photographs said to show a UFO (unidentified flying object) of classic saucer shape. Many people claim that some UFOs have a cosmic origin, but this is still very much in doubt. UFO sightings have occurred increasingly on a worldwide scale since the beginning of the Space Age in the late 1950s, which may or may not be a coincidence.

Top left: Some astronomers have begun searching for signs of extra-terrestrial intelligence (SETI). They not only listen for intelligent radio signals from the heavens, but also beam coded messages towards Sun-like stars in the hope that other beings might pick them up. This coded message, sent from the giant Arecibo radio telescope, includes information about the double-helix structure of DNA (which is essential to life on Earth), the Earth's population and the human form.

Fact or Fantasy?

Building cities that lie between the Earth and the Moon may be only the beginning of the thrust into space. Slowly but surely people will venture farther and farther afield, looking for suitable sites where the human race can continue to expand. To begin with, we will look at our nearest planetary neighbours in space – Mars and Venus. Of all the planets these are the two that are most like the Earth, though they are still very different from it. It is thought that in time both might be made suitable for human habitation. The other planets are not at all suitable. Mercury is so near the Sun that it is far too hot for life, as we know it, to exist. The planets beyond Mars – Jupiter, Saturn and so on – are far too cold. Also, with the exception of Pluto, these outer planets are almost entirely made up of gas and liquid gas.

The Red Planet

Of all the planets, we know most about Mars, which is often called the Red Planet because of its reddish-orange colour. Mars lies relatively close to us and has been visited by a succession of robot space probes since the mid-1960s. These probes have photographed the whole of the planet's surface as well as its two tiny moons, Phobos and Deimos.

In 1976 two American Viking probes softlanded on the surface, took close-up pictures of the rock-strewn rust-coloured landscape and even searched for life in the soil. For centuries Mars has been regarded as the planet most likely to support its own life. But the evidence from these probes now suggests that this is very unlikely.

Mars is very similar to Earth in two respects. It has nearly the same length of day, 24½ hours. Its axis is tilted by nearly the same amount, 24°, which means that it experiences seasons, like the Earth. But these seasons are nearly twice as long as those on Earth, because the Martian year is 687 Earth-days long. Mars' seasons are not marked by the growth and decay of plant life as they are on Earth, since no such life exists there.

Mars' Atmosphere

Mars has an atmosphere, but it is very thin and made up mainly of carbon dioxide. The planet could not retain a thicker atmosphere because it is too small and its gravity is too weak. Its diameter is only about half that of the Earth. There is no life-giving oxygen in the atmosphere, but there is a little water vapour which occasionally forms clouds. The polar caps on Mars contain quite a lot of water frozen as ice, together with dry ice or frozen

Left: This could be the site of one of the first planetary bases on the Martian Moon, Phobos. From tiny Phobos (or its brother satellite Deimos) astronauts could descend to explore the parent planet. Eventually the whole satellite might be converted into an enormous spaceport.

Below: Nine planets circle around the Sun, forming the major part of the solar system. This diagram (not drawn to scale) shows them in order going out from the Sun. The planets vary greatly in size, from Mercury which has less than half the diameter of the Earth, to Jupiter which has 11 times Earth's diameter.

carbon dioxide. There is much evidence from photographs of the surface that great floods once occurred on Mars.

It is possible that at some time in the past Mars had a much thicker atmosphere containing oxygen. This would have helped to keep the planet warmer than its present sub-zero temperatures. The presence of water, a thicker atmosphere and a warmer climate might have made the planet suitable for life of some kind to exist.

Mars base

Mars is nearly, but not quite, suitable for humans to live on. However, it is near enough, and early in the 21st century the first people will probably land on the planet to prepare the way for a permanent base there. These early landings would be similar to the exploratory Apollo landings on the Moon in the late 1960s and early 1970s.

The experience which space engineers would have gained during the building of colonies (page 73) could be put to good effect, and the Martian base would grow rapidly. The early arrivals would be engineers and miners who could at once begin mining to extract the raw materials necessary for construction. There seems to

This interplanetary cruise vessel, of enormous dimensions, has entered orbit around Venus, and winged rocket craft are being despatched from it to disperse algae into the swirling atmosphere below. This is the first stage of a scheme which would rid the planet of its heavy, suffocating atmosphere of carbon dioxide.

be an abundance of iron oxide ores on Mars, which means that iron could be cheap and plentiful. The rocks could provide the raw materials for making glass and concrete, used in construction. The combined oxygen locked in minerals in the rocks might be released by chemical processing. The polar caps could be 'mined' to provide ice for drinking water and irrigation.

Home from Home

Equipped with iron, concrete, glass, oxygen and water, people would be able to create an enclosed 'home from home'. As in all space colonies, the limited raw materials could be endlessly recycled and there would be little waste. By building gigantic greenhouses people in space cities might be able to grow their own food. There would not be the problem of the 14-day long nights and days as on the Moon bases, but there would be the problem of weaker radiation from the Sun. Even on the planet's equator, where bases would be sited, the sunshine is very much weaker than it is on Earth because Mars lies nearly twice as far from the Sun. So artificial electric lighting would be used in the greenhouses for most of the time. Electric power for the bases could be generated from nuclear plants rather than from solar power plants for the same reason.

Veiled Venus

Our other planetary neighbour, Venus, lies inside the Earth's orbit and comes closer to Earth than Mars does, occasionally approaching to within about 42 million kilometres (26 million miles). After the Sun and Moon it is the most brilliant object in the heavens. It would seem to be suitable for colonization since it has a thick atmosphere and is nearly the same size as the Earth. But in reality Venus is very different from the Earth.

The planet is permanently covered by clouds, and the atmosphere contains no oxygen but is made up almost entirely of carbon dioxide. This heavy atmosphere creates what is called a greenhouse effect. It traps the Sun's heat like a greenhouse does, with the result that the planet is even hotter than Mercury. The temperature at its surface can reach 450°C (842°F) – hot enough to melt tin, zinc and lead. Because the atmosphere is so dense, it exerts a pressure on the surface 100 times greater than the atmospheric pressure on Earth.

Clearing the Clouds

However unpromising Venus seems for colonization, some space scientists believe that they may be able to convert the planet into a second Earth. They would seek the assistance of some of the most primitive living things on Earth, the single-celled

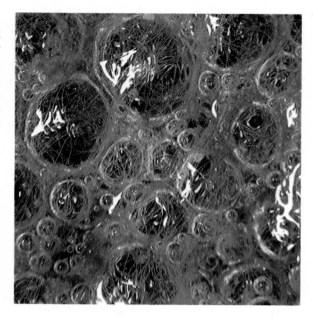

Blue-green algae like this are abundant on Earth and, genetically altered, could mark the beginning of the colonization of Venus. They would consume the carbon dioxide in the atmosphere, while at the same time producing oxygen.

As the atmosphere of Venus gradually lost its carbon dioxide, it would become lighter. There would be less of a 'greenhouse' effect, and the planet would start to cool down. Eventually, centuries later, the clouds would roll away and the Sun would shine on Venus at last.

blue-green algae. These convert carbon dioxide into food using the energy of sunlight. Like all plants, they give off oxygen as a by-product.

The idea is to inject rocket-loads of these algae into the atmosphere of Venus and let them go to work. The first stage of the plan would be to despatch to Venus a large inter-planetary ferry ship carrying a fleet of small rocket craft. The ferry ship would go into orbit round the planet while the rocket craft make repeated sorties to distribute the algae throughout the atmosphere.

A New Earth?

The algae would begin to reproduce rapidly, eventually clearing the atmosphere of carbon dioxide while providing it with oxygen. Gradually the atmosphere would lighten, allowing more of the hot trapped solar energy out. The planet would begin to cool. In time, measured in centuries rather than in decades, the water vapour in the atmosphere would condense and fall as rain. As the rain hit the surface, it would evaporate immediately and bring about further cooling. This effect, repeated over many centuries, could change the surface of Venus into a humid swamp. Then would be the time for human beings to appear on the scene to begin to build a 'new Earth'.

Shifting the Asteroids

During the centuries it would take for Venus to become habitable, space travellers may explore farther into the region beyond Mars, to the asteroids. These are lumps of rock which orbit the Sun between Mars and Jupiter in a broad band or 'belt'. The biggest asteroid, Ceres, has a diameter of some 1000 kilometres (620 miles) but most of them are very much smaller. Many hundreds of thousands are thought to exist.

Very far-sighted scientists think that eventually we could use the asteroids as raw materials for industry and construction. The asteroids could be blasted apart into a convenient size and then propelled by advanced nuclear and ion rockets into the vicinity of the Earth's orbit. There, they would not only be mined, but would be developed as self-contained orbiting 'city-states'. It has been suggested that these would eventually be arranged around the Sun in a broad belt, at roughly the same distance as the Earth and orbiting in a similar way. This arrangement is called a Dyson sphere, after the American scientist who suggested it. Professor Dyson thinks that such a sphere might be the hallmark of an advanced stellar civilization. When all of the asteroids have been used, it may even be

Although we are beginning to run short of essential raw materials on Earth, there is no shortage of them elsewhere in the solar system. One day other planets and their moons will be mined for the ores we require. So will the asteroids (right), which may well be moved into the vicinity of the Earth.

84

possible to dismantle the giant planets Jupiter and Saturn to obtain the raw materials for more city-states.

On to the Stars

If all the planets are colonized and adapted, and the whole solar system reshaped, what then? People may not stop with their development of the distant planets but make the next giant leap forward to the stars. Ours is not the only planetary system in the universe, and some of the nearer stars may well have planets which resemble the Earth. If we can eventually find them human beings may ultimately spread throughout the galaxy and perhaps even venture to other galaxies. But how can we travel to the stars, let alone search for suitable planets when we get there?

The closest star is over 4 light-years away, so a round trip to it would take over 8 years even if we could travel at the speed of light. At present, rockets can travel from the Earth at speeds of only about 50 000 kph (30 000 mph) – about $\frac{1}{22\,500}$ the speed of light. So a round trip to the nearest star would take nearly 200 000 years!

Novel rocket engines have been proposed that use beams of light as rocket exhaust. These so-called photon rockets could theoretically reach a speed close to that of light. Another ingenious idea is a kind of interstellar 'ramjet'. The sparse gaseous matter that exists in outer space would propel the proposed craft and it would be accelerated by means of a nuclear fusion reactor.

Science Fiction?

Many theories about the future of space travel might sound like science fiction. But they come, not from fiction writers, but from serious scientists. However sceptical we may be about a future in space, we should not forget that, not so long ago, the idea of spacecraft travelling to the Moon seemed beyond our wildest dreams.

The establishment of bases on the planets must await the development of new propulsion technology, for voyages of tens of millions of kilometres must be undertaken. Nuclear, ion or even photon rockets could provide the means when they are fully developed. All kinds of interplanetary cruise vessels will be designed – some capable of landing, others not. The satellites of the planets will provide convenient bases for exploratory expeditions.

A Better World

Many of the changes that will have taken place by the 21st century have already begun. We have started to find ways to solve many of the problems of the last few decades.

The prospects for people who live in the 'developed' world are good, but for the thousands of millions who live in the 'underdeveloped' parts of the world, the projections made in this book are sometimes inappropriate. The problems and needs of the Third World will be very different. Our responsibility towards poor countries must remain undiminished, and care must be taken to ensure that the mistakes we have made in the past are not also experienced by poorer nations as they progress towards industrialization.

Human Needs

There are hopeful signs that solutions to problems in the future will increasingly be based on human needs and expert advice. Experiments in Scandinavia and Japan, for instance, show that people tend to work better when they are allowed to make some decisions about how they organize their work. In the Swedish car industry, the monotony of the assembly line has been replaced in some factories by small teams of four to seven workers who build the car from start to finish, instead of just being 'cogs in a wheel'.

In the 21st century it is likely that more people will share the responsibility for making decisions so that machines can be used to advantage and the organization of the work becomes more personal and, therefore, more satisfying. Thanks to improved and highly flexible communications systems, it should be relatively easy to find out, in advance, what people think of proposed plans which will concern them and may alter the conditions they work in.

Expert Advice

Governments can also benefit from a different attitude to the problems that face them. Traditionally, they have relied on intuition rather than science when making decisions. But in the last 50 years the governments of industrialized countries have used the expertise of academics like economists, psychologists and sociologists more and more. These experts offer valuable knowledge and advice to many Western governments.

Whatever changes are made in the ways in which people reach decisions, it is certain that the world of tomorrow will be different. But it will still be recognizable.

Left: The solar furnace at Odeillo, France.

Most of the world, as we know it, has developed as a result of human needs, and these, like human beings themselves, will be much the same in the future as they are now. What will make the years from 2000 onwards so different from the present is that people will benefit from revolutionary technologies that are developing now.

A New Way of Life

The world of tomorrow should have an abundance of energy from sources such as the Sun and nuclear fusion. We should have learned how to conserve energy rather than waste it. We should have learned, too, how to take care of our environment so that the damage which has resulted from industrialization can, to some extent, be made good.

There will be enormous technological changes, and these will be developed more and more quickly. It took more than 100 years for the steam engine to be used throughout the world, almost 50 years for the petrol engine and nearly 30 years for the aeroplane. The most significant invention of recent years is the electronic computer. It is unusual because it extends our intellectual power rather than our physical power, like most inventions. The computer, particularly in the form of the microprocessor chip, promises rapidly to transform our way of life. Already, it has altered the way we communicate and has begun to eliminate tedious jobs. It has also become a valuable tool for scientific research and long-term planning.

Automation has for years been something many people suspected. They were afraid they would lose their jobs and machines would completely take over. But the robot devices which will become even more common in the next few decades will mean that men and women will do different, and, in many cases, more interesting jobs. As we have seen, automation should also release people from an eight-hour factory day so that they can have a more satisfactory and leisurely life-style.

Your World of Tomorrow

The technological advances of the next few decades are likely to bring about the most striking changes in the quality of life. Most people will continue to live in large cities, but these may well be arranged into small communities like villages.

Most of you who read this book will be a part of the world of tomorrow. It is the world you and your children will live in. If we use our new discoveries wisely and plan ahead thoughtfully, that world should be an exciting place.

Glossary

Binary system Number system using 2 as a base. Only two symbols, 0 and 1, are required to express a number. The decimal system uses the base 10 and requires the symbols 0-9.

Catalyst Substance used to speed up or slow down a chemical reaction. The catalyst itself is not chemically changed by the reaction.

Cosmologist Scientist who specializes in cosmology, the study of the universe as a whole.

Cybernetics The study of communications and control mechanisms in living things and in machines.

Electrolysis Method of breaking down certain chemical substances by using an electric current. The current passes through a solution of the substance and splits it up into simpler substances.

Gene Hereditary unit in chromosome (part of the living cell) that passes on characteristics from one generation to another in plants and animals.

Holography Method of reproducing 3-D pictures using a laser beam instead of a camera.

Hydroponics System of growing plants in a chemical solution without soil.

Hypersonic Speed greater than Mach 5. Mach numbers are used to describe the speed of an object moving through the atmosphere in relation to the speed of sound at the same height. The speed of sound, expressed as Mach 1, varies with temperature and therefore with height.

Ion Atom or group of atoms carrying an electric charge. The electric charge is caused by the loss or gain of electrons. An atom with fewer electrons than protons is positively charged; one with more electrons than protons has a negative charge.

Isotope Forms of an element with the same atomic number (number of protons in the nucleus) but with different atomic weights. The variation in weight is caused by different numbers of neutrons in the nucleus.

Laser Microwave amplifier which produces an intense narrow beam of light that is monochromatic (single colour) and coherent (all its waves are in step).

Magnetometer Instrument for measuring the strength of magnetic fields.

Megawatt 1 000 000 watts. The watt is the unit of electrical power.

Mesquite Spiny American shrub belonging to the mimosa family.

NASA National Aeronautics and Space Administration, the US government agency responsible for space exploration.

National grid Network of wires and cables distributing electric current to all parts of the country.

Oscilloscope Electronic instrument which shows electric signals as traces on a fluorescent screen.

Plasma Very hot gas used for nuclear reaction experiments. Plasma has equal numbers of positive and negative ions.

Pulsar Tiny star that gives out high-energy radiation, usually in the form of radio signals, at very regular intervals.

Quasar Mysterious star-like object outside our galaxy. Quasars are powerful sources of radio waves and light.

Retro-rocket Rocket fired by a spacecraft in the direction of travel to slow it down.

Scintillation counter Device for detecting and counting the number of alpha particles coming from a source. Alpha particles are the helium nuclei given out by some radioactive elements. Surveyors use scintillation counters in their search for radioactive minerals.

Seismograph Instrument for recording earthquakes. In seismic surveying, prospectors cause small explosions that send shock waves through the ground. They use a seismograph to record the passage of the waves and then analyze the resulting wave patterns to find out what kind of rocks lie below the surface.

Sonar System that uses high-frequency sound waves to locate unseen objects. A sonar device transmits sound waves which are then reflected as echoes by an object. The time taken by the waves to reach an object and return indicates the object's position.

Spectroscope Instrument for producing and examining the wavelengths (colours) contained in a single light beam.

Stratosphere The second-lowest zone of the atmosphere. It extends from about 12 km to 80 km above the Earth's surface and includes the ozone layer.

Thermionic valve A vacuum tube in which one of the electrodes is heated so that it emits electrons. The electrons can flow in one direction only, i.e. the valve becomes a semi-conductor.

Third World The nations of the world are sometimes divided into three groups: the economically developed non-communist countries; the communist countries; and the poorer developing countries, the Third World.

Turbine Motor in which a shaft is rotated by the impact of steam, air or water onto the blades of a wheel. Turbines have no pistons or cranks.

Turbogenerator Electric generator powered by a steam turbine. Most conventional power stations have turbogenerators.

Index

ACKNOWLEDGEMENTS

Picture Research: Tracy Rawlings and Elizabeth Rudoff

Photographs: endpapers Tony Stone Associates; title page Paul Brierley *(left)*, John Hillelson/Howard Sochurek *(right);* contents page ZEFA; 13 Bergström and Boyle Books Ltd *(above),* The Post Office *(below;* 14-15 Pilkington Brothers Ltd; 16 Paul Brierley *(above),* International Society for Soiless Culture *(centre),* ZEFA *(below left),* Australia News and Information Service *(below right);* 18 Sarah Tyzack; 19 ZEFA; 20 South American Pictures/T & M Morrison *(above),* NOAA *(below);* 20-21 NASA; 22 Seaphot; 25 Syndication International; 26 EMI Medical Ltd; 27 Alan Hutchinson *(above),* John Hillelson/Howard Sochurek *(below);* 29 Ford Motor Company; 31 Ford Motor Company *(above),* Blau Punckt/Bosh *(below);* 32 The Post Office *(above),* Daily Telegraph Colour Library *(below);* 34 Mick Csaky; 38 John Hillelson/Dr. Georg Gerster; 40-41 ZEFA; 44 Boeing Aerospace Company/Nasa; 45 UKAEA *(above),* NERSA *(below);* 46 Courtesy Commission of the European Communities; 47 Lawrence Livermore Laboratory *(above left),* Photri/ZEFA *(above right),* Lawrence Livermore Laboratory *(below);* 49 Kennecott Copper Corporation; 51 Deepsea Ventures Inc/E D Blekenship; 53 Paul Brierley *(above),* Courtaulds Ltd *(centre),* Image in Industry Ltd *(below);* 54 Datsun *(above),* Ford Motor Company *(centre),* Fiat *(below),* 55 no credit *(above),* OELD, Paris *(below);* 56 Paul Brierley; 57 Paul Brierley; 58 Courtesy Intel Corporation; 59 Paul Brierley; 60 Tony Stone Associates; 61 Picturepoint Ltd; 62 ZEFA *(above),* Picturepoint Ltd *(below);* 63 Photo Library International; 64 ZEFA; 65 Daily Telegraph Colour Library; 66 J Allan Cash *(above),* William Macquitty *(below);* 67 Forestry Commission *(left),* Natural History Photographic Agency/Philippa Scott *(right);* 69 Macmillan's Childrens Books; 70 NASA; 75 Californian Institute of Technology; 76 CERN; 77 CERN *(above),* CERN/colour treatment by Patrice Loiez *(below);* 78 Max Planck Institute for Radio Astronomy, Bonn; 79 ZEFA; 83 Oxford Scientific Films; 88 John Hillelson/Dr. Georg Gerster.